DECODING HUMANITIES

HUMANITIES FIRST EVER SELF-HELP BOOK

GURU TAHANGURIYA

Copyright © 2025 Guru Tahanguriya

Made with ❤ on the Notion Press Platform

www.notionpress.com

To all those who love and support us unconditionally, I dedicate this book to you.

Contents

Preface

I chose to open this book with a simple truth: *"Sometimes, it's not the hard stuff that trips us up, but the easy stuff we overlook."* And here's why.

Every year, I receive countless messages from humanities students, frustrated that despite their efforts, they struggle to achieve good grades.

But when we talk, we find out it's not the hard stuff they're struggling with, it's the basics. They're not getting the simple things right, and that's what forced me to write this book.

If you're expecting to learn something entirely new from this book, I'm sorry to disappoint you. Everything written here is likely something you already know. These are things you've known for years, yet still struggle to implement correctly.

Your parents scold you daily to be more active, use your mobile less, keep the house clean, drive slowly, and help them. It's understandable if you get irritated, wondering why they keep telling you things you already know. But deep down, you understand the truth: even though we know what's right, we often fail to follow through.

Despite pretending not to listen to our parents, their reminders echo in our heads each time we do something wrong. Whether we acknowledge it or not, these constant reminders impact our lives.

Similarly, consider this book a reminder - a reminder you need, even though you may already know everything. I hope that after reading this book, you'll be on the right track and become a top performer.

This book is structured in a way that allows you to dive into any topic at any time, without needing to follow a specific order. Even if you find reading this book boring or feel like you already know everything, please keep reading. You won't be disappointed by the end.

Happy reading!

1. Humanities/Arts Stream

This section provides an in-depth understanding of the Humanities/Arts stream, exploring what sets it apart from other fields. It helps you reflect on whether this stream aligns with your interests and goals, offering clarity to make informed decisions.

Why Humanities/Arts Stream Is Different?

A common mistake students make after opting for the humanities/arts stream is assuming that humanities stream subjects will be similar to the social science subject they studied in lower classes.

This assumption is not entirely accurate. Although the subjects may be the same or similar, there is a vast difference in their approach and complexity.

You need a completely different mindset to tackle the challenges of the humanities stream, which we will discuss further in this book.

Another distinctive feature of the humanities stream, compared to other streams like commerce, PCB, and PCM, is the freedom students have to form their own opinions.

While two plus two will always equal four; concepts like rights, democracy, and society can have different interpretations for each student.

This is one of the best aspects of the humanities stream. Instead of rote memorisation, you learn, grow, and evolve.

Are you the Right Student for the Humanities/Arts Stream?

Well, everyone can excel in almost any field if they are ready to put in the required effort. However, some traits make a student particularly well-suited for the humanities stream.

A student who loves to read about history, politics, geography, and more, who finds joy in understanding the past, envisioning possible futures, and contemplating our role in building a great society, will love this stream.

This stream demands time, effort, patience, and resilience. One of the biggest misconceptions about the humanities is that only students who are bad at academics choose this subject, but this is utterly untrue.

In reality, students who do not follow the herd mentality and have greater aims and interests often pursue this stream.

A person who loves technology and science more might not initially enjoy this stream, but it is possible to stay connected with science and technology even after choosing humanities; it just requires some extra effort.

After reading this, if you feel happy, great, you are a perfect fit. But if you don't feel that way, let me assure you that you are still a great fit, because after reading this book, you will understand everything about the humanities stream.

"The difference between ordinary and extraordinary is that little extra."

— Jimmy Johnson

Stand Strong Against the Noise

Once you choose Humanities, many people will start criticising your decision, saying it's the worst stream to take. They'll call it a stream for weak students, claim it doesn't suit you, will say it has limited scope, and that you'll end up regretting your choice. After hearing all this, your heart starts pounding, and you begin to doubt your decision.

So, the question is, how do you deal with it?

Here's the answer.

First of all, you need to realise that society is changing rapidly, and so are opportunities. Yes, years ago, Humanities was seen as a stream chosen by weaker students, and the scope was limited, but that's no longer true.

Before taking anyone's opinion seriously, **ask them two things**, **1.** Are they themselves from a Humanities background, and if not, how do they know so much about it? Are their views based on assumptions or random conversations?

2. And if they are from Humanities, are they aware of how the landscape has changed? Did they give their best, or are they judging the stream based only on their own failures?

I hope you see the point; most opinions people hold are baseless.

You've got two ears, listen from one and let it pass through the other. If someone says something useful, reflect on it and look for solutions. But regret, it won't take you anywhere.

"Taking a different path doesn't mean you're lost; it often means you're brave enough to walk where few have dared."

Common Myths About Humanities

The Humanities stream is often surrounded by myths that make students doubt their decisions. These misconceptions are not only outdated but also deeply misleading.

One of the most common myths is that **"only weak students take Humanities."** In reality, Humanities demands a strong command of language, critical thinking, emotional intelligence, and the ability to understand society, skills that are not just relevant but essential in today's world.

Visionaries like Dr. B.R. Ambedkar and Shashi Tharoor, global icons like Malala Yousafzai, celebrated economists like Amartya Sen, and renowned historians like Romila Thapar all come from a Humanities background. Clearly, this stream is chosen by thinkers, leaders, and change-makers, not by weak students.

Another myth is that **"there's no future or jobs in this stream."** This couldn't be further from the truth. Humanities opens doors to many career options: civil servant, lawyer, journalist, content writer, editor, researcher, psychologist, sociologist, teacher, public policy, advertising, marketing, human resources, event management, public relations, media production, museum curator, art historian, librarian, foreign service officer, diplomat, social worker, NGO professional, counsellor, mental health specialist, graphic designer, animator, filmmaker, photographer, business consultant, entrepreneur, management, corporate communications, translator, linguist, language teacher, economist, political analyst, policy advisor, fiction writer, non-fiction writer, environmental studies, sports management, tourism, event planner, social media manager, SEO specialist, content strategist, brand manager, fundraiser, corporate social responsibility, international relations, international development, cultural affairs, government researcher, scientific writing, etc. ***Phew!***

Some also claim that **"it's all theory and no skill"** which shows a clear lack of understanding. Humanities students develop some of the most transferable and future proof skills - public speaking, research, writing, logical reasoning, empathy, and social analysis.

These skills power careers in media, diplomacy, politics, education, and beyond. Take Yuval Harari for example, the author of Sapiens, used his understanding of history and philosophy to reach millions across the globe.

A related belief is that **"Humanities students aren't successful."** Success is subjective, but if it means making a difference, gaining recognition, or building wealth, then Humanities graduates have done it all. Barack Obama studied Political Science. Arundhati Roy, who won the Booker Prize, studied literature and architecture. Amitabh Bachchan has an arts background. Even industrialists like Ratan Tata value the liberal arts for shaping better leaders. From authors and diplomats to journalists and educators, Humanities graduates have shaped ideas, institutions, and entire generations.

Finally, there's the myth that **"Humanities students don't earn much money."** Income in any field depends on smart work, not just the stream. Corporate lawyers, professors, psychologists, and even content creators with Humanities backgrounds earn exceptionally well.

In truth, Humanities is not a fallback stream. It's a foundation for leaders, creators, and thinkers. If pursued with clarity, consistency, and creativity, it can lead to immense success, both personal and professional.

"Just because a path is less crowded doesn't mean it leads nowhere - sometimes, it leads exactly where you're meant to be.

Build Your Own Way

Not every road is paved in gold,
Not every story has been told.
Step by step, come what may,
Brick by brick, build your way.

The stars won't light the path for you,
The winds may change, the skies turn blue.
Dreams aren't found, they're made today,
With courage sharp, carve your way.

No maps, no rules, no borrowed skies,
Just open roads and daring eyes.
Trust your soul, come what may,
You were born to build your way.

2. How to Get Started?

"The secret of getting ahead is getting started."

- *Mark Twain*

In this section, I guide you through the essential first steps in your Humanities journey. From selecting the best resources and channels to managing projects and understanding the role of your school, I cover everything you need to build a strong foundation.

Additionally, I will help you create a timetable that optimises your time and ensures a structured approach to your studies.

Finding the Right Resources

Good resources play a significant role in the humanities stream. Having the right resources is crucial if you aspire to be a top performer.

But the biggest challenge students encounter is the abundance of resources in the market and online platforms, with each claiming to be the best, leading to confusion.

Allow me to share a secret of high achievers: *you only require a few quality resources to excel in this stream.*

Let's delve into each type of resource one by one:

Main Book: In most humanities subjects, the main book is the NCERT. Your exams for 11th, 12th, and CUET will be based on NCERT. Not a single question will come outside the NCERT books. However, please note that in a few subjects like Economics and Physical Education, NCERT alone may not suffice; you may need additional reference books recommended by your school teachers to complete your syllabus. Remember, without a thorough understanding of the main book, other resources may prove ineffective.

Question Bank: After completing a chapter from the main book, you need to review all the important questions from that chapter, and for this, you'll need a good question bank. A question bank will help you identify key questions, assist in revision, and aid in answer framing. A good question bank contains high-quality questions based on the latest syllabus. However, mistakes in question banks are common, so always cross-check answers with the main book.

Notes: There is nothing better than making notes for revision, as it is scientifically proven that this aids in better retention. We will discuss this later in the book.

Past Year Questions: Purchasing books containing past years' questions is also a valuable resource to understand the exam's level and prepare accordingly. Good question banks usually cover past year questions (PYQs), but there are also separate books available that only include question papers from the past 5-10 years.

Sample Papers: After completing the syllabus, solving sample papers is crucial. It helps in revision, time management, and answer framing.

By now, you might be wondering how to make the best use of resources. Don't worry, we'll explore that in detail later in the book.

Resources alone aren't enough; it's the will, decisions, and persistence that create success.

Figuring Out the Best Channels

YouTube is filled with channels, and new ones emerge every single day. Becoming an educator on YouTube doesn't require a degree, making it easy for individuals without expertise to start their own channels.

Every year, I receive hundreds of messages from students who subscribed to the wrong YouTube channels. These channels often fail to explain concepts clearly, resulting in decreased academic performance.

Therefore, it's crucial to know how to assess a channel effectively.

The Wrong Approach

Judging a channel solely by its views, subscribers, and video rankings on YouTube can sometimes be a big mistake. Subscribing to a channel based solely on someone else's recommendation is also not the best approach. As a student, you are easily influenced. Educators can sway you by creating highly energetic videos and presenting themselves in a favourable light.

The Right Approach

There are certain traits of a good channel. A reputable channel always provides accurate information and remains connected with its audience. It shows improvement over time and is willing to acknowledge and rectify mistakes.

When creating syllabus-related videos, they cover all necessary topics thoroughly without skipping anything. Their actions speak louder than their words. The best way to evaluate a channel is by comparing it with others.

For instance, when studying a particular chapter, read the corresponding book first, then watch videos from various educators on YouTube to determine which one offers the most valuable content. Remember, shorter video duration doesn't necessarily indicate better quality; many students make this mistake.

"Happiness is when what you think, what you say, and what you do are in harmony."

— Mahatma Gandhi

Headaches of Projects

In the humanities stream, one of the biggest challenges is creating numerous files and assignments. One of the best things you can do is to create these files and assignments as early as possible.

Avoid waiting until the last minute. Students who procrastinate often struggle to manage projects and assignments along with final exams.

Here's a pro tip: always choose straightforward topics from your main textbooks for your files. This will help you avoid difficulties during practical exam vivas.

Role of School

In the humanities stream, two types of students typically enrol: those who attend school regularly and those who do not. We cannot overlook the pivotal role that schools play in this regard.

Schools keep students updated about the syllabus and any new changes or updates in the curriculum. Regular exams and studies in school enforce a disciplined study routine and contribute to our improvement.

Therefore, if you are a regular student, attending school is highly beneficial as it provides valuable learning opportunities.

However, if you are a non-attending student, it becomes essential to keep yourself updated. You can stay informed by maintaining friendships with students who attend school regularly or by periodically checking for updates yourself.

Additionally, it's crucial to remain consistent and avoid wasting time if you are not attending school.

"School is not just a place to learn, but a place to discover who you are."

How to Make a Perfect Timetable

Crafting a perfect timetable is one of the most important tasks if you aspire to become a top achiever. A well-structured timetable helps maintain consistency and ensures we are always aware of what to study and when.

An effective timetable is one that is easy to follow, practical, aligns with your daily routine, and can be easily adjusted as needed.

Before creating a timetable, several considerations should be taken into account. You should be familiar with your daily routine, be well-informed about upcoming exam dates, assess the remaining syllabus, identify areas requiring revision, recognise topics needing thorough study, and pinpoint challenging areas. A great timetable should effectively manage all subjects.

Most Practical Way

The best way to form a practical timetable is to use a simple formula:

total remaining chapters divided by total remaining days.

Let's understand this with an example. Rahul is a class 12th student and his board exams are approaching soon. He needs to complete his syllabus somehow in just 25 days. He doesn't know what to do and wonders if he will be able to complete the syllabus on time, so he decides to create a timetable.

First, he writes down all the chapters in his syllabus for each subject. Suppose his subjects are History, Political Science, Sociology, Physical

Education, and English. He finds out that the total number of chapters across all subjects is 75.

Next, he categorises these chapters. Out of 75, he has already completed 30 chapters thoroughly and does not need to study them again until exam time. In 15 other chapters, he only needs to do a revision, and 30 chapters are still left to be studied.

So, in total, 30 chapters are done, and out of the remaining 45 chapters, 15 need revision and 30 require complete study.

Now, he uses the formula:

total remaining chapters divided by total remaining days.

$45/25 = 1.8$, which he rounds off to 2 chapters per day.

This means if he studies 2 chapters per day, he will be able to complete his chapters within 25 days.

Next, he uses the MQ+R formula: -

- M for Main Book

- Q for Questions

- R for Revision

For all the chapters he has already done, he either does nothing or simply does a quick revision of his notes. For the chapters that require revision, he uses one-shot videos, notes, or practice questions to complete them. For the chapters that are not yet done, he studies everything from the main book and uses all necessary resources mentioned in the previous chapters of this book.

This is how he completes his entire syllabus without any headache or confusion. This timetable helps him organise everything efficiently.

Trust me, a good practical timetable can do wonders.

Creating a Personalised Study Plan

A question may have come to your mind: How much should I study every single day from the very start? Let's try to understand it. When considering how much to study each day, we should not include online classes, school, or coaching sessions, as these are not in our control. What is in our control is how much time we dedicate to self-study from the free time we have.

Here's a simple exercise: Ask yourself, is attending school, coaching, or online classes enough for my studies? Do you feel confident with your progress? If the answer is yes, then your main aim should be to revise what you've learned in those places and focus on clearing any backlogs, if you have any. But if the answer is no, either because you don't feel confident or you don't attend school, coaching, or online classes, then you should follow the formula I mentioned earlier.

Formula: *total remaining chapters divided by total remaining days.*

Ask yourself how many days you want to complete your syllabus in, how many chapters there are, and how many extra days you'll need for revision. Once you have that, you can calculate your daily targets.

For example, let's say I attend classes and go to school but still feel underconfident. I'll make a plan: I need to complete the syllabus in 60 days and set aside 30 extra days for revision, totalling 90 days. If there are 60 chapters, I'll divide 60 chapters by 60 days, which gives me a goal of 1 chapter per day (excluding revision days for now). I will then follow the same MQR strategy I mentioned earlier in this book.

Once the syllabus is complete, I will use the same formula for revision. Since I've kept 30 days for revision, and there are 60 chapters, my revision target would be 2 chapters per day.

What if you want to complete the syllabus while also revising the chapters you've already covered? In that case, you can use the formula twice - once for syllabus completion and once for revision. I hope you're getting my point: you can create your own set of daily targets based on your situation. Just act smartly.

"Success is the sum of small efforts, repeated day in and day out."

— Robert Collie

The Value of Time

Time is a river, swift and deep,
It moves so fast, it never sleeps.
A moment lost can't be regained,
A gift once gone, can't be contained.

So use it well, with heart and mind,
For fleeting hours are hard to find.
In every tick, a world awaits,
Don't let it slip through careless gates.

3. Humanities Secrets

"We are not meant to stay the same. We are meant to grow, to evolve, to become better than we were yesterday."

-   Beau Taplin

This section unveils the hidden factors behind success and failure in the Humanities stream. I will explore why only a few students excel and the common pitfalls that lead to setbacks.

From mastering note-making and retention techniques to understanding NCERT, I will share essential study strategies.

Learn how to tackle different question formats, balance multiple subjects, and optimise your study hours.

I will also address common misconceptions, such as the "school exams scam" and the truth about books, videos, and courses, helping you navigate your academic path with clarity and confidence.

Why Only a Few Students Succeed?

Every single student has pondered this question: Why do only a few students succeed while the majority do not? What makes some students special?

To be honest, there is no single answer to this question. We all face different challenges and have different ways of dealing with them. What worked for one person does not necessarily mean it will work for you as well.

However, there are a few habits that are consistently found among top students - what we call *"toppers' secrets."*

Let's discuss them one by one:

1. Power of Consistency

Let's assume the total number of chapters across all subjects is 110. Realistically, your total chapters are likely closer to 100, but let's stick with 110 for this example. Now, assume it takes you 3 hours to complete one chapter. To finish 110 chapters, you would need 330 hours, which translates to approximately 14 days if you studied non-stop. Overwhelming, right?

However, if you study for 3 hours a day, you can complete these 330 hours in 110 days, which is around 3 and a half months. This demonstrates the power of consistency. Studying a little bit every day adds up significantly over time. You can complete your entire syllabus in roughly 3-4 months without any rush or problems.

Now, consider this: if you have fewer chapters and study more than 3 hours a day, what will be the outcome? You guessed it, you'll finish even faster!

2. Good Relationship with Teachers

Most top students maintain great relationships with their school teachers. Regardless of personal feelings, they recognise that teachers possess the experience and authority that can ease their school life and improve their results. For example, having good relationships can lead to better marks in practical exams and viva, as well as access to free resources and personal guidance.

3. Friendships

Friendship is not a business; we make friends who understand us and share a similar vibe. However, you will notice that top students often maintain good relationships with their intelligent classmates because they receive mutual benefits.

For example, a day before an exam, you might get a call from a friend saying they haven't studied anything yet, and you may both laugh and waste time. In contrast, a top student will receive calls from friends focused on important discussions, such as reviewing key topics or revising together. Do you see the difference?

4. Self-Awareness

Some understand better when someone teaches them, while others prefer self-study. Some study at night, while others love to study in the morning. Some enjoy watching movies for entertainment, while others prefer playing games. *What works for you works for you.* The problem arises when you start to copy others, especially those you perceive as superior to you. A fish cannot fly, and a monkey cannot live underwater. Understand yourself and work accordingly. Most toppers are aware of what works for them and what doesn't.

5. Self-Fulfilling Prophecy

It's human psychology that we try to maintain a good image that people have of us. A topper behaves like a topper; they participate in events, are disciplined, never give anyone a chance to point at them, and act like they are already a topper. Their act of behaving like this forces them to give their best, whereas students who are not toppers never complete their work on time, delay things, and have a weak mental image of themselves.

6. Right Resources

Toppers always use the right and limited resources. They do not rely on everything available, and this makes a big difference. The right resources have already been mentioned earlier in this book.

7. Pre-Planning and Routine

Toppers pre-plan almost everything. They know what to study, when to study, and how to study. They have a clear plan for when they will complete their syllabus and when they will start revision. They think ahead and do not leave things for the future.

They follow a routine and *stick to it.*

"The future belongs to those who shape the present with purpose and action."

8. Smart Work

Toppers are smart; they spend their time wisely. They only participate in activities that help them grow. They maintain good relationships with their teachers and befriend smart students. They complete their projects and assignments ahead of time, allowing them to focus on studies. They do not waste time scrolling through social media. They do everything to minimise their efforts while maximising their output.

9. Intrinsic Motivation

Toppers possess a burning desire to achieve their goals. They work diligently with a clear purpose, relying less on external motivation. The inner drive within them compels them to persevere even during challenging times.

10. Self-Confidence

You'll seldom hear a topper express doubt about their abilities. Internally, they harbour a strong sense of self-assurance, firmly believing in their capability to excel.

11. Creating Own Environment

Toppers usually have friends and people around them who are equally motivated, encouraging them to study harder and challenging them to excel. Together, they create a positive environment, striving to steer clear of negative influences.

Ask yourself: Who is around you? Are they people who objectify women, or those who talk about morality? Are they people who want to be successful, or people happily investing their parents' hard-earned money?

You are the average of the five people you spend the most time with.

– Jim Rohn

12. Mistakes

Most students repeatedly make the same mistakes. You often hear classmates saying, 'I can't finish exams on time,' 'I always procrastinate and then suffer,' 'I forget what I study,' or 'I can't concentrate,' but they seldom make efforts to improve. Many students are aware of their mistakes but refuse to accept and work on them. This reality is both sad and true. Toppers consistently work on their mistakes and learn from them.

13. They Compete, But They Don't Compare

Comparison is one of the biggest factors contributing to student failure. Many students compare themselves with others and subsequently feel sadness or jealousy. Toppers greatly admire students who surpass them and compete with them, but they rarely engage in comparison. We are all unique and always will be.

"Where competition thrives, compassion withers, for they cannot bloom in the same soil."

14. They Know What is Important

I receive messages from students even a week before exams, asking about the syllabus, chapter weightage, paper patterns, and more. These things are most important, and you should be aware of them months before exams. I have never seen a topper behaving this way.

15. Dealing with Failure

Toppers don't let their failures determine their future; they overcome them. Many students who score lower marks often assume they can't become toppers and let their failures dictate their path. However, a true topper never does this. They keep fighting and never lose hope.

Reasons of Failure

There are many reasons for failure and inability to score good marks, depending on our life and situations, but some of them are very common and crucial to avoid.

1. Resources

We all need food and water to survive, but what happens if we only eat junk food and drink dirty water? You all know the answer: we will fall ill and various diseases will affect us. The same happens with resources. We all need books and videos to score good marks, but when we consume whatever, we get without analysing if it's right or not, our grades start to fall. I have already mentioned resources earlier; do read it carefully.

2. Copying What Toppers Do

There are two things to understand. First, no one tells you the real story, especially topper students. They might say they study only one hour, but in reality, it may be eight. They might say their syllabus is incomplete, but in reality, they may be doing revision for the second time. We can never know their real life. Second, why copy others? We all have different lives, and copying does not make any sense. Always get influenced by people doing better than you but don't copy them. Create your own life path always.

3. Lack of Consistency

Videos like *"How to Complete Syllabus in 5 Days"* will never work. You can rarely beat someone who has been consistent throughout the session. Start from today and study daily. The majority of students who fail admit that they were not consistent.

"Day one or one day, you decide."

4. Lack of Self-Belief and Small Thinking

If you do not trust yourself, if you do not believe that you can become a topper, you never will. I have never seen a highly underconfident person succeed. Trust yourself and work hard. Suppose if you think you can only jump two feet, will you ever try for four? If you think you can only score 70%, will you put in the effort enough to score 100%? **Never!**

5. Repeating Mistakes

If you don't learn from your mistakes, you will never become a topper. School exams are for you to learn from your mistakes so you won't repeat them in final exams and competitive exams. If you don't know how to frame answers, if your speed is slow, if you make silly mistakes, if you read questions wrong, etc., work hard on such mistakes and avoid repeating them. There will never be a day when you don't make mistakes, they are a part of life and it's okay, but when you repeat the same mistakes many times, it becomes a problem.

"The only real mistake is the one from which we learn nothing."

— Henry Ford

School Exams are a Scam

You must have admired many of your school seniors who always topped their classes and were teachers' favourites. However, not all of them performed exceptionally well in board exams. Why?

The answer is simple: *school exams are a scam!*

In many schools, the question papers are not up to the mark, and even if they are, the grading done by teachers is often poor.

Teachers frequently award more or less marks than deserved, and partiality sometimes comes into play. The big problem here is that students who score high marks in school consider themselves highly intelligent, while those who score lower marks believe they don't deserve to excel.

As a result, both types of students suffer. The high scorers prepare less due to overconfidence, and the low scorers don't give their best effort.

Another issue is that students are unable to identify their exam mistakes because of this flawed system. Consequently, they fail to improve.

What's the solution then?

Stop blindly trusting school exams. Instead, conduct self-analysis and study the answer sheets of board exam toppers to understand how they write in exams and answer questions.

Initial Hard Work

Let me predict the future: a majority of students will feel stressed and overwhelmed a week before exams because their syllabus will be incomplete, and the resources they created, like notes and book highlights, will be insufficient. They will not know what to do.

But why will this happen?

Because of the lack of initial efforts. Many students have the habit of delaying important tasks and procrastinating.

For example, they might think, *"This topic is difficult; I'll do it later,"* or *"Creating detailed notes is important, but I'll do it later."* They might believe, *"Highlighting the book is a good idea, but I'll do it later."*

And that "later" never comes.

Toppers never do this; they understand the value of initial efforts. One of the biggest keys to success as a student is to give high efforts initially.

From the very first day, start giving your best. Do not skip anything for the future.

Trust me, this initial push of hard work will give you many peaceful nights in the future and will also save you from many regrets.

Note Making

Making notes is one of the most important tasks for humanities stream students.

Humanities subjects often have lengthy textbooks, and it's not efficient to repeatedly invest time in reading them. A better approach is to create notes, which allows you to revise the syllabus more quickly once you have a solid understanding of the syllabus.

Now comes the question: *How do you make amazing notes?* The answer is quite simple. Your notes should cover all the important points, but they shouldn't look like you've just copied the entire book. Keep them precise and in your own style.

If you like using short forms, acronyms, mnemonics, or symbols - go ahead. If you prefer making flowcharts, do that. It's completely up to you. The only goal is that your notes should be so concise that they make revision quick and easy.

Many students make the mistake of copying everything from the book in the name of note-making. That's not effective. Remember, your notes should work for you. It's perfectly fine if others can't understand them, as long as you can.

I always emphasise note-making because it's scientifically proven that writing helps us remember things better.

One great way to organise your notes is to divide your notebook into sections - for example, dedicate a few pages for dates, some for important names, some for flowcharts, a section for full forms, and another for previous year questions (PYQs), etc. This method will help you create your own master set of notes for revision.

"Writing crystallizes thought and thought produces action." — Paul J. Meyer

How Not to Forget

The biggest problem for almost every single student is forgetting what they learn. Nothing comes to mind when they try to recall, even after spending many hours studying.

This phenomenon happening a few days before an exam is completely normal due to stress and anxiety. However, if it happens regularly, it's a dangerous situation.

Here are some tips that will surely help you:

1. Think Before Moving Forward

Sometimes we are so engrossed in reading or watching an explanation video that we forget we are merely going through the motions without truly understanding. After finishing a topic, ask yourself: was I just watching or reading, or was I also understanding? If the answer is yes, move to the next topic. If no, revisit the topic until you understand it completely.

2. Quick Revision is Not Always Great

Sometimes, we revise a topic or chapter immediately after completing it, but this isn't always very effective. When we learn something new, it stays fresh in our mind for a short time. A quick revision right after studying might make us feel confident, but we can still forget the information later, just like we often forget the names of new people we meet. That's why revising again after a few hours or days is equally important.

3. Make Notes and Put in Effort

It's scientifically proven (known as the **"generation effect"**) that putting in your own efforts while studying, like making notes, increases retention levels and helps you remember better.

4. Revise Regularly

No one remembers everything they learn or read. Frequent revision is crucial, so revisit each chapter as many times as necessary until you feel confident. There are no shortcuts.

5. Use Tricks and Mnemonics

When it comes to memorising data and facts, tricks and mnemonics can be very helpful. Create mnemonics to aid your memory when you struggle to learn something.

For Example:

- Trick to Remember SAARC Countries

- Mnemonic: **MBBS PAIN**

1. M- Maldives 2. B- Bangladesh 3. B- Bhutan 4. S- Sri Lanka 5. P- Pakistan 6. A-Afghanistan 7. I- India 8. N- Nepal

Data and Facts

Data and facts are the heart and soul of the humanities. Most of the questions in 11th and 12th class exams, as well as the CUET exam, will be related to data and facts. If you have a strong command over these, success is within your reach.

However, the biggest problem with data and facts is that they are not easy to learn. If not given importance from the beginning, they can lead to significant trouble.

The best solution is to start learning them from the very beginning. Every time you come across something related to data and facts in your book, highlight it with a different colour highlighter and also create separate notes for them.

This way, during the final days before the exam, you can easily revise without the hassle of finding them in books. Also, try to arrange the data in chronological order so you can link information easily and understand it better.

Do not forget to pay attention to timelines and boxed information provided in books, as they are important for the CUET exam.

Review the separate notes you created for data and facts regularly, and soon, you'll be able to recall them even if someone wakes you up from sleep.

How to Understand NCERTs

Many toppers do not accept this, and I don't know why, but NCERT books are not easy to understand. So much detail is given in so few pages, making it difficult to understand every single line. Apart from this, there is a lot of data and facts written, and the language of the book is not easy. Thus, many students, even after reading it multiple times, do not understand anything.

But this problem can be solved, and it's not as difficult as you might think.

Firstly, whenever you are in school or attending online classes, pay close attention to what your teachers are explaining. This way, when you read the NCERT book, it won't feel completely new, you'll already be familiar with much of it.

If you find reading NCERT difficult or boring, watching YouTube videos can be a good alternative. However, be very careful, not every channel covers the NCERT line by line properly. If you watch videos from a channel that skips lines, misses important points, or explains things incorrectly, it can create major problems for you later.

There is also an activity you can do: first, read a topic from the book and try to understand it, then watch a video and see if you understood it correctly or if you misinterpreted the NCERT. This helps a lot to improve our understanding capabilities.

If there is any word or line in the NCERT which you don't understand at once, after watching videos or googling that word or sentence, write its easy explanation in the NCERT itself so that when you read it again, you can see the meaning or understand it even if you forgot. You can use AI tools like ChatGPT, Gemini, etc., to understand difficult lines in a better way.

Also, remember that when you read NCERT or watch videos more than once, you understand better because the first time, we unintentionally miss out on many things. So, revision is important.

Do whatever you want, but never ever skip NCERT. If you skip NCERT, you will never be a topper - harsh but true.

Question and Answers

Suppose a question appears in a science paper, and you observe the answers of all the students who answered it correctly; you will notice that all the answers are almost identical. However, this is not the case in the humanities stream. Every single answer will be different yet correct. This means you need to have a comprehensive knowledge of the syllabus to design your own answers.

In this stream, understanding the question is very important before you answer it. As you already know, writing answers in points is always appreciated, and for that, you need to understand the books in detail. When you know the syllabus very well, it becomes much easier to make flowcharts, subheadings, and points.

The best way to understand answer framing is to analyse toppers' answer sheets, which you can download from Google for free. See how they write and design their answers.

Many students with complete knowledge of the syllabus score very less marks because they just don't know how to frame perfect answers.

How to Write Perfect Answers

In the Humanities stream, questions are usually divided based on marks - ranging from 1 to 8 marks. Each type requires a different approach to answer writing.

Basic Structure for Long Answers (4-8 Marks):

To write a solid answer, keep the following structure in mind:

1. Introduction

2. Flowchart

3. Subheadings using the same points from the flowchart

4. Conclusion

Now, let's understand how to approach questions based on their marks.

1–2 Marks Questions

You don't need to follow the full structure here. A simple, direct answer is enough.

For example, if the question asks, *"What is the definition of X? (1 mark)"*, you simply write the definition. If the question asks, *"Mention two features of X (2 marks)"*, you simply write two features.

---

*Keep this rule in mind: for any point or paragraph, the **maximum marks you can get is usually 2**.*

Let's understand this through examples.

Example 1

Question: Name any two members of the Y community. (1 mark)

Here, you will get **½ mark for each name**, so writing two names will get you full marks.

Example 2

Question: Name any two members of the Y community. (2 marks)

Now, each name will carry **1 mark**, so again, writing two names will give you full marks.

Observation: The value of each point or paragraph varies depending on the marks allotted, even if the question remains the same.

Example 3

Question: What do you mean by Y? or write a short note on Y. (2 marks)

Here you need to give **two valid points** about Y as the question is for **2 marks**. Either write one paragraph (worth 2 marks, by adding two valid information in the paragraph) or, preferably, write two clear points.

Writing in points is usually a better choice.

The key takeaway is: Always read the question carefully, check how many marks it carries, and structure your answer accordingly.

3-8 Marks Questions

Example: What do you mean by R? Mention any two features. (3 marks)

This question has two parts:

- Meaning of R = 1 mark

- Two features = 2 marks

So don't write a whole page on the 'meaning' as it is only for 1 mark, just a short paragraph will do. Then write two points for the features.

The key takeaway is: If the question has multiple parts, try to break it down based on the marks. For example, if a 4-mark question asks two things, it likely means each part carries 2 marks. Plan your response with this division in mind.

For questions above 3 marks, it's important to follow a structured format.

Use:

- **Introduction**

- **Flowchart**

- **Subheadings** (based on the flowchart)

- **Points under each subheading**

- **Conclusion**

Example: 6 Marks Question

Question: Describe any three consequences of Z event.

Here's how to break it down:

Each consequence = 2 marks (3 x 2 = 6 marks total)

Answer Structure:

1. **Introduction** (Briefly explain Z event)

2. **Flowchart** (List the three consequences)

3. **Subheadings** (Use same headings from flowchart)

4. **Points** (Under each subheading, write at least 2 points to justify the 2 marks)

5. **Conclusion**

This method ensures your answer is well-organised and meets the marking criteria.

What if the Question is Difficult?

If the question is too challenging to create flowcharts or subheadings, simply write your answer in well-structured points. That is completely acceptable and still effective.

What if Time is Limited?

In 3–5 mark questions, if you're short on time, you can skip the introduction, conclusion, and flowchart, unless they are specifically asked. Try to include subheadings, if possible, but if even that isn't feasible, focus on writing clear, relevant points directly.

Bonus Tip: Always Write Extra

Adding extra relevant points increases your chances of scoring full marks and shows better understanding.

I know this particular topic was a bit much to take in, so I recommend reading it again for better understanding.

To Sum Up:

General Rule -

- Structure your answers based on the marks allotted.

- Maximum marks for one point/paragraph are usually 2 marks.

1–2 Marks Questions -

- Keep answers short and direct.

- 1 mark = 1 valid point or definition.

- 2 marks = 2 valid points.

- Prefer writing in points rather than paragraphs.

3-8 Marks Questions -

- Break down based on marks.

- Follow a structured format.

- Distribute your content based on mark allocation

Multiple Choice Questions

MCQs (Multiple Choice Questions) are of great importance because they are commonly asked in school exams, board exams, and most notably, the CUET, which is completely MCQ-based.

Many people find MCQs difficult to answer due to confusing options and the challenge of memorising data and facts. However, with the right approach, answering MCQs correctly can be quite easy.

Firstly, you need to have a comprehensive understanding of the syllabus and memorise the related facts and data thoroughly. Whenever you complete a section of the syllabus, underline or write down every significant fact and all relevant data you encounter.

By 'fact,' I mean any point in the book that is concrete, unchangeable and has its own value, such as *"India is the 7th largest country by area"*, this is a fact. Similarly, *"The laws of motion were given by Newton"*, this is also a fact. 'Data' refers to dates, names, full forms, timelines, etc.

You will be surprised to know that most of the MCQ questions asked in the CUET and other exams are predominantly based on facts and data.

The majority of students struggle with MCQs because they do not focus on data and facts from the beginning and tend to procrastinate. It is not feasible to learn all the dates and facts in just a few days; it requires consistent revision and effort over time.

Balancing Subjects

One of the biggest mistakes students make is to postpone studying either the easiest or the most difficult subject, thinking they have enough time, but that time never comes.

Balancing all subjects is extremely important for several reasons:

Firstly, school exams do not differentiate between easy and difficult subjects. When exams take place, all subjects will be tested, and almost the same chapters will be covered.

Secondly, if you start studying an easy subject from the beginning, there is a high chance you will score full marks because it's easy and you have given it sufficient time.

Thirdly, if you do not tackle difficult subjects from the start, you won't be able to handle them later. Even if you try, all your time might go into that one subject, leaving other subjects with insufficient preparation time.

Always balance all subjects. By balancing, I do not mean preparing for each subject every single day. It is best to focus on one or two subjects per day, but ensure you give importance to each subject.

"Life is a balance between holding on and letting go."

– Rumi

Best Time to Study and How Much to Study

What is the best time to study? The actual answer is that there is no single best time. We are all different, some of us are morning birds, some are night owls, and some are a mix of both. Some prefer to study for longer durations at once, while others like to take short breaks periodically.

Always remember, *"what works for you works for you"*; there is no need to copy anyone else's routine or schedule. However, there is one crucial thing to keep in mind: **your energy levels**.

Our body and mind's energy fluctuates throughout the day, and you should be aware of when you feel the most energetic and focused. That time is precisely when you should study, although many of us fail to do so.

If you feel highly energetic at 5 PM, you should study at that time. Unfortunately, many students waste this peak energy period by sleeping, calling friends, going out, etc. They then try to study when their energy levels are at their lowest, forcing themselves to stay awake despite feeling sleepy. This is counterproductive.

Become aware of your energy levels. Additionally, pre-plan your daily study targets as discussed in the timetable section.

Suppose your target for today is two chapters. If you can complete them in one hour, that's fine; if it takes six hours, that's also fine. The time spent doesn't matter as much as achieving your target or goal. Align your daily targets with your daily energy levels for optimal results.

Holidays and Vacations

I have often told humanities students that the best use of holidays and vacations is to complete pending assignments, projects, and school work. These tasks can be time-consuming and become significant hurdles when exams are near. The earlier you complete them, the less stress you will feel later.

If you have already completed your pending work, you can focus on completing your syllabus or doing revisions.

Try to stay ahead of your school curriculum so that when a topic is taught in school, it serves as a revision for you while other students are encountering it for the first time.

Always aim to work smart.

Books, Videos, and Courses Scam

This is the most dangerous scam in the humanities stream, where students are manipulated and later suffer greatly.

1. Books Scam

There are many books available that are not suitable for preparation. These poor-quality materials are often promoted by influencers who are paid to endorse them. As a result, students are misled into believing that these materials are the best. Do not blindly trust influencers.

Here's a secret: every single session, influencers, including us, receive emails from almost all publishers. The worse the quality of their material, the better the offer they make. It is completely our choice to promote them or not. I never reply to any brand that is not up to the mark, but unfortunately, 99.9% of influencers do the opposite and promote the brand that offers the most money.

They make false claims in their videos, stating that the video is not promoted and that they personally recommend the book, but that is all a lie.

There is a dark side behind the camera. Not all the influencers you consider your "bhaiya," "didi," or "teacher" genuinely care for you; some are just here for business, hiding behind a mask and pretending to care. Understand this.

Pro Tip - After reviewing so many books, I have concluded that there is not a single book without mistakes; it is common. Therefore, when purchasing a book, focus on the quality of the questions it provides, not the answers. Always cross-check the answers with the main textbook.

"Don't trust the surface; even still water can conceal a storm."

2. Videos Scam

Before writing this book, I analysed many videos from top humanities creators and, I am sorry to say, many videos had numerous mistakes. Wrong information was provided, and some of these teachers are so famous, yet they still do this.

One big mistake in an explanation video can be very harmful to students.

Always match videos with the syllabus and cross-check explanations from the main book. Do not watch videos that skip topics or explain them incorrectly.

A video ranking on YouTube does not mean the video is good. Before trusting any channel, analyse that channel carefully. Many channels promote their videos as the best in the whole world, but again, it's a lie.

3. Courses Scam

Purchasing a course is not bad, but purchasing courses without properly analysing them is. Do not purchase out of fear that everyone else is buying it, so you should too.

Only purchase if you need it and if it is worth your time and money. I will repeat it again: if the person who created the course says it's the world's best, that does not mean it is. Understand that!

P.S. - No one will ever tell you what I just told you in this part of the book. But for me, 'honesty is the best policy.'

"Integrity is doing the right thing, even when no one is watching."

— C.S. Lewis

4. Exam Days

"Believe in the hours you've studied, the effort you've put in, and the strength within you, because success is not just about what's written on paper, but the confidence you carry into the exam hall."

- Unknown

In this section, I provide practical strategies to help you excel during exams. Learn how to effectively interpret your date-sheet to plan your preparation, and discover the right approach to attempting your exam papers.

I also share last-minute revision techniques, tips for staying calm and focused on exam day, and the importance of solving sample papers to enhance your performance. These insights will equip you with the tools you need to tackle exams with confidence and efficiency.

Understanding the Date-Sheet

Before every exam, you receive a date-sheet listing all exam dates and the gaps between exams. Analysing the date-sheet is crucial for effective preparation.

Weeks Before Exams

As soon as you get the date-sheet, you should prioritise subjects with unfinished syllabus and those with minimal preparation gaps. Otherwise, you risk losing marks.

Few Days Before Exams

In the days leading up to the exams, focus solely on the subject of the first exam, giving it your complete attention to avoid potential problems.

When There Is Less Gap Between Exam

When there is little to no gap between exams (1-2 days), concentrate on revising and reinforcing what you already know. Avoid starting new topics. Also, check the syllabus weightage and pattern before preparing.

When There Is a Big Gap Between Exams

With a longer gap between exams, you have two options. If other exams have shorter gaps, you can use the initial days of the break to prepare for them. Alternatively, if the upcoming exam is difficult or the syllabus is incomplete, use the entire gap period for preparation and revision. Do not waste time thinking you have enough days.

The Last Exam

Many students lose focus before the last exam. Don't make this mistake; the last exam is as important as the others. Give it your best effort.

In stillness, I find my way,
While noise and doubt drift far away.
One thought, one step, one steady flame,
And all the world feels just the same.

Right Way of Attempting Paper

Humanities Subjects

If you ask me, I always suggest students start their paper with the longer questions that carry more marks, and then move on to the short and very short questions.

The reason for this is that at the beginning of the exam, we have enough time to think and write well-constructed answers, which is crucial for scoring full marks.

As the exam progresses and time becomes limited, we tend to panic, and our minds may not process information properly, leading to silly mistakes.

For example, a short question like *"When was XYZ formed?"* can be answered in seconds, even if your heart is racing. However, a long question like *"Mention the features of the XYZ"* requires a calm mind to answer effectively. Do you get my point?

Language Subjects

In language subjects, let's suppose Section A is for reading comprehension, Section B is for grammar and writing skills, and Section C is for questions and answers.

Here, I suggest two approaches:

1. Do Section C first, then Section A, and finally Section B.

2. Alternatively, start with Section A, then Section C, and finish with Section B.

During the reading time, read the passages carefully. If you find them easy, do Section A first. However, some students prefer to start with Section C because the chapters are fresh in their minds at the beginning of the exam. This makes it easier to attempt the question-and-answer section without worrying about forgetting the answers or being unable to frame them properly.

It is suggested to do Section B, which involves grammar and writing skills, at the end because it takes time and there is no single correct answer. For instance, if there's a question to write a letter, every student will write it differently, which can lead to spending too much time on it and not having enough time for other sections.

Therefore, it is best to leave it for last so that you know how much time is left and can divide it accordingly for Section B.

P.S. – Before following these strategies, try them on sample papers to see if they work for you. You are free to attempt the paper in your own way as well.

Final Revision

When you are revising any chapter for the final time, start with the questions and answers and PYQs (Previous Year Questions).

Attempt them on your own. If you answer any question correctly, that's perfect. If you don't, read and learn the answer. Additionally, revisit the topic from which the question originated, because there is a high chance that if another question comes from the same topic, you won't be able to answer it.

Proper knowledge of that topic is crucial.

During the final revision, focus only on the topics you understand. Do not start preparing anything new; otherwise, you won't have enough time to review the topics you already know, and new topics won't get enough attention to be well-prepared.

Reviewing data, maps, cartoons, images, facts, etc., at the end is very important so that they remain fresh in your mind, helping you score full marks.

Exam Day Tips

1. Smile when you wake up on the exam day. Starting your day with a smile sets a positive tone. Worrying won't change the outcome, it only makes things worse, so smile instead.

2. Just before exams - revising dates, facts, maps, cartoons, names, full forms, members of organisations, headquarters' names, book names, character names, etc., is crucial. You get marks with minimal effort by doing this.

3. Focus only on what you know, not on what you haven't prepared well.

4. Forget the past; your past won't decide your present or future.

5. Repeat five times: *"My name is [your name] and I can do it."*

**No dream is too far, no peak too high,
For those who toil and never sigh.
With every step, with sweat and grace,
Hard work will win the silent race.**

How to Solve Sample Papers

You should target a minimum of two sample papers for each subject, and these two papers will be solved in completely different ways. The remaining papers can be used for practice or reading, which will be explained later.

Solving the First Sample Paper

Set a timer for 20 minutes more than the actual exam time. For example, if the exam duration is 3 hours, set a timer for 3 hours and 20 minutes.

Use this extra time to write down your mistakes and areas for improvement on a separate sheet of paper while you attempt the paper.

For example, if you notice you gave extra time to MCQs, which was not a good idea, write it down. The goal is to analyse your performance and identify your weaknesses.

Solving the Second Sample Paper

Use the insights gained from the first paper to improve your performance in the second paper. Do not repeat the mistakes you made the first time and see how much you have improved. For this paper, there is no need to set extra time.

Remaining Sample Papers

After attempting two sample papers, if you have time, you can solve as many papers as you want until you feel confident and stop repeating mistakes. If you don't have time, you can simply read the remaining sample papers or solve them quickly without setting the full timer.

Additional Tips

To improve your exam performance, gradually reduce your mistakes through consistent practice, maintain a stable approach by not changing your paper-solving strategy close to the exam, and ensure you have a comprehensive understanding of the entire syllabus before attempting sample papers.

A seed once hid beneath the ground,
In silence deep, without a sound.

Afraid, unsure, it stayed below,
Yet slowly felt the urge to grow.

It broke the dark to touch the light,
Now stands a tree, in fearless height.

For even in the darkest place,
Begins the rise of strength and grace.

5. Ending Humanities

"An investment in knowledge pays the best interest."

- Benjamin Franklin

I've shared everything I needed to about the Humanities stream, and now it's time to move beyond it and explore other areas that will contribute to your growth. In this section, I'll address some final questions you may have regarding the Humanities.

Is Class 11th Important?

Many students ask whether Class 11th is important, and the answer is yes, it is, in many ways.

Students who prepare well for the Class 11th syllabus often find Class 12th easier. By putting in the effort in 11th, such as making notes and completing assignments, you develop the strength to handle pressure situations and build strong work habits.

Class 11th also offers various opportunities. You should focus on participating in as many activities or events as possible, making new friends, building good relationships with teachers, learning from seniors, and preparing for competitive exams like CLAT if you wish to.

Remember, it's the second-to-last year of your school life, so give your best and live it to the fullest.

Be so well-prepared for Class 12th that you don't face any new challenges when you enter it.

11th Class vs Board Exams vs CUET

In my opinion, when you are in class 11th, you should focus solely on the class 11th syllabus. There is no need to prepare for the CUET exam at this stage; that can wait until you enter class 12.

Now, addressing the concerns of class 12 students: they often ask if the value of board exams has decreased after the introduction of the CUET exams. The answer is both yes and no. You can no longer secure admission to top institutions through high percentages in your 12th-grade board exams; you need a good score in the CUET exam. However, board exams still play a crucial role.

The syllabuses for class 12 and the CUET are almost same and NCERT-based. Therefore, if you prepare well for your board exams, you are automatically preparing for the CUET exam as well. The key difference is that the board exams include both objective and subjective questions, while the CUET exam is entirely objective. Both are based on NCERT, so thorough preparation using NCERT books will ensure you score well in both your board exams and the CUET.

Do not take your board exams lightly. After they are over, focus more on the remaining syllabus not covered in the board exams and on objective questions.

I have never seen someone score high marks in the board exams but low in the CUET. If you prepare well for your boards, you will be prepared for the CUET as well.

The best approach is to also start preparing for Language Test and the General Aptitude Test (only if it is compulsory for the university you are thinking of applying to) from the start of class 12. Focus more on data and fact mentioned in NCERT books so that preparing for the CUET becomes easier. Learn NCERT thoroughly.

If you are not from CBSE and are from any other board where NCERT is not followed, please try to cover NCERT content whenever you get time. Otherwise, you may find the CUET exam challenging.

PS - Whenever CUET results are tied, board exam scores are considered to determine who ranks higher and secures the seat. Similarly, for degrees like MBA, a good board exam result is important.

Practicals

Practical exams are a crucial part of the humanities stream. Scoring well in them is essential if you want to become a top student. By keeping a few simple things in mind, you can easily score high in practicals.

Always prepare your files as early as possible, ideally during summer vacations. If you are late, no problem - do it as soon as you can.

Always select easy topics for your files and practicals that are part of your syllabus. Do not try to impress teachers by selecting difficult topics.

Suppose you select a topic for your file that is part of your syllabus. In that case, the external examiner, who is also a teacher, will be well aware of the topic because it is part of the syllabus. This increases the chances that the external examiner will ask questions only from your file and, in some cases, also from the syllabus, keeping you on the safer side.

However, if you select a unique topic or one that is not part of the syllabus, there is a chance that the external teacher may not know much about it. Even if they do, they won't know what you have written in your file since they don't have time to read it in detail, so they might ask any question from anywhere. This can put you at a disadvantage.

If you think you have enough time for revision, remember that the whole month (most often January) is spent preparing for and giving practical exams, so you won't get much time for final exam preparation. Don't wait until the last month for preparation; practicals consume a lot of time!

Motivation, Consistency, and Knowledge

I've interviewed many humanities toppers. There are some traits that are consistently common among all the toppers.

First, toppers rely more on intrinsic motivation than extrinsic. This does not mean they don't need someone to motivate them, but it means that most of the time, they don't need external motivation because they are already motivated.

The reason for this intrinsic motivation is **PURPOSE**. Toppers know what they are doing and why they are doing it. Having a purpose is most important; it keeps them full of burning desire and drives them to act and give their best efforts.

Second, of course, is **CONSISTENCY**. Drop by drop makes the ocean. No one is born a topper, and no one can become one in a few days. Consistent hard work is crucial.

Studying for four hours per day is far better than studying for eight hours one day and then not studying at all for a week.

As Aristotle said, "We are what we repeatedly do. Excellence, then, is not an act, but a habit."

Third and last, they *SEEK KNOWLEDGE* every single day and are curious. They don't believe they know everything; instead, they believe they know nothing and keep looking for more wisdom.

As Confucius said, "The man who asks a question is a fool for a minute, the man who does not ask is a fool for life."

Career and Scope

In India, choosing the Humanities/Arts stream for your education opens up a world of diverse career possibilities. Despite being sometimes overlooked, this stream offers plenty of opportunities for those who enjoy creativity, thinking critically, and understanding different cultures. Let's explore some career options available to those who pursue humanities and arts education in India.

Career Options After Humanities/Arts Stream in India

After completing the Humanities stream, a variety of career options open up across diverse fields.

You could choose to work as a journalist, content writer, copywriter, editor, or social media manager, focusing on communication and media.

If you're interested in analysis, careers like research analyst, market research analyst, or data scientist may appeal to you.

Those interested in public service can aim for civil services (IAS, IFS, IPS), political analyst, diplomat, or policy advisor.

For a career in helping others, roles like social worker, psychologist, career counsellor, and NGO worker are highly rewarding.

Creative professionals can thrive as an artist, fashion designer, graphic designer, animator, filmmaker, actor, choreographer, or music director.

If education excites you, becoming a teacher, professor, or educational consultant could be fulfilling.

Law offers career paths such as lawyer, legal advisor, court reporter, or paralegal.

Tourism management, event planning, advertising, and branding are great options for those looking to work in the corporate or hospitality sectors.

Further, political scientist, historian, archaeologist, philosopher, sociologist, anthropologist, and economist are roles for those passionate about research and academia.

Humanities graduates can also become museum curators, cultural advisors, policy advisors, or pursue roles in public administration, international relations, or foreign languages.

With so many career options, the key is to align your strengths and interests with the path that brings the most satisfaction and growth.

In India, the humanities and arts stream offer a wide range of career paths, each with its own unique opportunities for growth and fulfilment. Whether you're passionate about teaching, writing, helping others, or preserving culture, there's a place for you to shine.

So, if you're considering a career in humanities or arts, know that your talents and interests can lead to exciting and meaningful opportunities in India's dynamic job market.

Remember, these are just a few examples of the many career paths available to those in the humanities stream.

So, as you embark on your journey, keep exploring, stay curious, and don't be afraid to carve out your own path. After all, in the vast landscape of India's career options, there's something for everyone to discover and pursue.

Additional Resources

This is the only topic in the entire book where I'll recommend my own Humanities resources, and that's because they're genuinely valuable.

Many of you already know that I run a YouTube channel called **'THE TWIN BROS – HUMANITIES'**, and I also have a dedicated app and website specifically for Humanities students. I want to share some of the amazing resources we offer on our channel that I believe will truly help you.

Explanation Videos: On our channel, you'll find detailed line-by-line explanation videos for chapters across many Humanities subjects for both Class 11th and 12th.

FPH Series: On our YouTube channel, we have the "Fasna Pakka Hai" series for Class 12. In this series, we cover all possible questions from the main book. Ask any former Humanities student, and they'll tell you how effective this series is. Every year, so many questions come from this series alone - just check the comments on these videos, and you'll be surprised by the success stories.

MCQs Series: For Class 12, we also offer an MCQs series, which is extremely beneficial not just for board exams but also for the CUET exam.

It's closely related to the FPH series, helping you strengthen your foundation.

Notes: We provide well-organised, concise notes tailored specifically for 11th and 12th Humanities students. It's all about making learning easier and more efficient for you.

Telegram Channel: Join our Telegram channel for a treasure trove of free resources. It's the most active Humanities channel on the internet, and you'll absolutely love it.

Live Classes: We also offer live classes on our website and app, which I truly believe are the best that you'll find. I'd bet on it!

Study Materials: On our website and app, you'll find a wide range of materials - answer writing videos, notes, sample papers, important PDFs, and more. It's a goldmine for Humanities students, offering both free and paid content to cater to every need.

Rapid Revision Series: One of our most popular series on YouTube is the Rapid Revision series, where we provide quick revisions of entire chapters, packed with solid notes. This is perfect for last-minute revisions or quick refreshers.

Channel: We call our channel **'Humanities ka Ghar'** because we want you to feel right at home. On our channel, you'll find everything, from in-depth explanation videos to revision content, guidance, motivation, and even topper interviews. Simply type **https://bit.ly/4aAFZHN** on google and you'll have everything you need in one place.

Application Name: The Twin Bros

Website: www.thetwinbros.in

"We must accept finite disappointment, but never lose infinite hope."

— Martin Luther King Jr.

Light of Hope

Hope is a spark in the darkest night,
A quiet whisper, burning bright.
Through storms and trials, it still remains,
A promise carved in golden flames.

6. Exploring CUET

What Is CUET?

The CUET UG Exam (Common University Entrance Test) is a national exam conducted by the National Testing Agency (NTA).

It is used for admission to undergraduate courses in various universities across India.

The exam started in 2022 to make the admission process fairer and reduce the need for different entrance exams for each university.

Before CUET

Before the introduction of CUET for admission to top universities, all you needed was a high score in the 12th board exams, something like 95% or more was enough to secure admission in universities like Delhi University.

However, that's no longer the case. Now, to get into such universities, you must appear for the CUET UG exam and achieve a high score.

CUET Syllabus

The syllabus hasn't changed much in recent years, it's almost the same as the Class 12 NCERT syllabus.

In a few subjects, there might be some extra topics, but for most, only the Class 12 NCERT content is included. So, if you're preparing for Class 11 and 12 sincerely, there's no need to worry about the CUET syllabus separately.

For example, in CUET 2025, deleted chapters of Sociology were included in the CUET syllabus. Similarly, topics from the Class 11 Economics syllabus were also part of the exam. However, in subjects like Psychology, Political Science, History, and others, only the Class 12 board syllabus was included.

CUET Exam Pattern

CUET exams are conducted either in CBT mode (Computer-Based Test) or using an OMR sheet, and sometimes even a mix of both.

The paper includes only multiple-choice questions (MCQs), and there is negative marking as well.

However, small changes are made every year, so it's always best to read the latest CUET UG information bulletin available on NTA's official website for accurate and updated details.

CUET Subjects

The CUET UG exam is divided into three parts: Language Test, Domain Subjects, and the General Test (GAT).

You can choose from various languages, domain subjects like History, Political Science, Economics, etc., and the General Test, which covers reasoning, current affairs, and basic math.

Not all sections are compulsory, it depends on the course and university you're applying to.

For complete and updated details, always refer to the official CUET website.

CUET Cutoffs

CUET cutoffs are usually quite high, so if you wish to get your desired course in a top college, it's best to aim for full marks. Even a single wrong answer can affect your chances of admission. This isn't to stress you out, just sharing the reality so you can prepare accordingly.

Admission Criteria

The admission criteria for each university can be different. While many universities accept CUET scores, that doesn't mean they all follow the same rules.

For example, in 2025, Delhi University required students applying for BA (Hons) to appear for **1.** three domain subjects and one language test or **2.** two language tests and two domain subjects. The General Aptitude Test wasn't compulsory.

In contrast, for the same course at Banaras Hindu University (BHU), the required combination was a language test and general aptitude test, and domain subjects were not needed.

Also, while many universities accepted any domain subject in CUET, Delhi University only allowed the subjects you studied in Class 12.

That's why it's always best to check the eligibility criteria of each university either on their official websites or on the NTA's official website to be sure.

Best Universities and Colleges

If you're a Humanities student aiming for quality education, some of the top universities in India include the University of Delhi (DU), known for its prestigious colleges like St. Stephen's, LSR, and Miranda House, and Jawaharlal Nehru University (JNU), highly respected for Political Science, Sociology, and History.

Ambedkar University Delhi offers interdisciplinary Humanities courses, while Ashoka University provides a world-class liberal arts education in a private setup.

Tata Institute of Social Sciences (TISS) is excellent for social sciences and psychology, and Christ University in Bengaluru is known for courses in Psychology, English, and Economics.

Banaras Hindu University (BHU) and Jadavpur University are also strong options with well-established Humanities departments.

These are just a few examples; India has many other universities that also offer excellent Humanities programmes.

Ultimately, the "best" university for you will depend on your career goals, financial situation, subject interests, location preferences, and other personal factors. Choose what aligns best with your path.

Always remember: It's the students who truly make a university great, not just the institution itself.

While top universities certainly offer immense opportunities and exposure, remember that success can be achieved from anywhere in the world.

All it takes is the courage and determination to give your best.

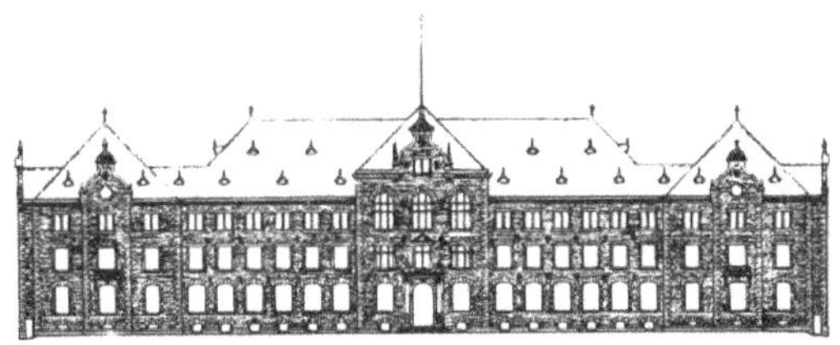

CUET Preparation Guide

The ideal way to prepare for the CUET is from the day you enter 11th grade. However, the approach in class 11 will be very different.

In class 11th, focus on doing your best, loving the syllabus, and reading the NCERTs as if they should stick in your brain. Enjoy 11th grade to the fullest.

When you move on to 12th, continue this approach but with ultimate focus and dedication. Read the NCERTs as many times as possible and practice MCQs. The amount of hard work you put in during 12th grade will definitely pay off in the CUET exam.

Once your 12th grade is over, you won't have much time for CUET preparation, usually just about a month. But honestly, this is enough if you've prepared well for 12th.

Now, your main aim should be to revisit the NCERTs thoroughly. In board exams, not every box, timeline, picture, or detail in the NCERT is important, but in the CUET, anything can be asked, even a single line that might be hard to notice without specs! So, read it thoroughly.

After that, practice as many MCQs as you can. Don't just practice, though, analyse the mistakes you make. Categorise the MCQs you get wrong, whether they involve dates, names, facts, or specific chapters. Once you identify these patterns, start focusing on improving them.

Never underestimate the power of mocks. Take mock exams so you won't panic during the actual test and will know how to manage tough situations and time. The more mistakes you make in preparation and learn from them, the better your chances of scoring well in the CUET.

As I've said many times before, NCERT books are the key to everything.

When it comes to the English and General Aptitude Test, if you think you're weak in these areas, start giving them some attention from 11th grade onward. If you're okay with them, focus on them from 12th grade.

One month won't be enough if you're weak in these areas. Prioritise basic math and English, with more emphasis on English, as the General Aptitude Test isn't compulsory in all universities.

If you start dedicating even a tiny fraction of time to these subjects from 12th grade, you'll be far ahead of the competition.

Also, make sure to give time to learning the elimination method. Even if you don't know the answer to an MCQ, this strategy can help you get it right.

The **elimination method** involves removing obviously incorrect options in multiple-choice questions to narrow down your choices. By focusing on the remaining options, you can make an educated guess even if you're unsure. It's a useful strategy to increase your chances of selecting the correct answer, as sometimes the wrong options still provide valuable clues or details.

Out of the four options, one is correct, but that doesn't mean the other three are useless. They still hold valuable information.

For example, when asked about the year a certain treaty was signed, one option will obviously be correct. However, the other options might refer to different treaties, providing years or other relevant details. So, focus on the incorrect options as well.

Don't worry too much, these strategies will come naturally to you once you start your preparation.

All the best!

The future waits with open skies,
A world of dreams, a place to rise.
With every step, we make our way,
Creating hope with each new day.

7. Mind Matters

"Your thoughts are the seeds. You can grow flowers, or you can grow weeds."

No amount of knowledge is truly useful if your mind isn't healthy and stable. So, in this section, I'll talk about mental health and share everything that personally helps me keep my mind grounded and happy.

Overthinking

Overthinking is something that has silently ruined millions of lives.

The constant mental chatter, strange dreams, morning headaches, loss of energy, anxiety, lack of focus, fear of the future, and worst of all, watching your overthinking slowly turn into reality.

The more you try to control it, the more intense it becomes.

You struggle, you fail, and a single question starts haunting your mind: *"I wish there was a way to overcome this. I wish I could just live and think like a normal human being."*

But how do I know all this? The answer is simple: *I was once a student who suffered deeply from overthinking.*

Now, the question is: how do we deal with it?

The solution lies in the very first line of this book:
"Sometimes, it's not the hard stuff that trips us up, but the easy stuff we overlook."

Dealing with overthinking isn't as difficult as it seems, once you understand what it truly is.

The first step is to realise the difference between **thoughts** and **thinking**.

"You don't suffer because of a thought. You suffer because you believe it."

— Byron Katie

As human beings, we have *no control over our thoughts.* On average, around 3,000 thoughts pass through our mind every hour. And we all know how negative some of them can be.

But thoughts aren't the problem, they come and go very quickly. The real problem begins when we grab hold of one and turn it into thinking.

We have no control over a thought, but we do have full control over thinking.

For example, a random thought crosses your mind: *"I might fail."* If you simply let it pass, it causes no harm.

But instead, you hold on to it:
"Oh no, what if I really do fail?"
"I might disappoint everyone."
"Maybe I'm not good enough."
"I wish I had done better with my life."
"I wish I hadn't wasted so much time…"

And just like that, a passing thought turns into a spiral of mental exhaustion.

But it doesn't end there, this constant overthinking leads to a deeper issue: **emotional imbalance.**

Our emotions are directly tied to our thoughts. Have you ever noticed how low you feel when someone says something hurtful? Now imagine doing that to yourself, over and over, by cooking up an entire meal of negative thoughts inside your head.

It leads to sadness, anger, frustration - sometimes all at once. And you find yourself saying, *"I don't know what's happening to me, but I don't feel okay."*

So, what's the permanent solution?

If you've read this carefully, you already know the answer: **Stop converting thoughts into thinking.**

And this only becomes possible when you stop giving unnecessary importance to the thoughts themselves.

"A thought comes uninvited. Thinking is when you serve it tea."

Whispers of the Mind

A thought appears, then fades away,
Like clouds that drift but never stay.
Some bring peace, some stir the night,
Some dim the soul, some spark the light.

They knock, unasked, at every door,
But you decide which ones explore.
Not every whisper needs reply
Just breathe, just watch, just let them fly.

This will take time, but you can do it.

Whenever you notice a negative thought, either ignore it or gently say to yourself: ***"I won't let this thought ruin my mind. I'll use my mind for something good instead."*** And you'll notice, the thought will begin to fade on its own.

This practice takes time, but it does work with consistency.

Here's another beautiful truth about thoughts:

You can't have two thoughts at the same time.

What does this mean? It means that if you consciously engage your mind in something meaningful or positive, negativity has very little space to stay.

Now, let's come to an important question:
Why do we get negative thoughts in the first place?

The answer isn't simple, it's a result of many factors: your environment, past experiences, life situations, and more. But here's the part that gives hope:

You can change the quality of your random thoughts over time.

How? By shaping your environment with your own hands.
Read good books.
Listen to uplifting videos.
Surround yourself with positive, grounded people.

And slowly, you'll start seeing your thoughts shift, just like how negativity disappears when you're playing your favourite game or doing something you truly love.

Overthinking is the illusion of understanding. We seek answers, yet the more we think, the more we distance ourselves from true peace, which lies not in answers, but in surrender.

Emotions

According to science, emotions are complex psychological and physiological responses to stimuli that influence our thoughts, behaviours, and perceptions. But in simpler terms, I believe ***emotions are the way our body expresses itself when words cannot.***

Here's the interesting part: our body is not great at differentiating between what is real and what is not.

For example, imagine you see a tiger, your heart races, your body panics, you run, and you feel exhausted. The tiger is about to eat your leg, and you scream - and then, suddenly, you wake up. *Oh, it was just a dream.* But you felt all the emotions as if it were real. Your body takes a few minutes to accept that it was only a dream.

The same thing happens in our daily lives. We often live in a constant state of fight or flight, and our emotions are not under control. The problem arises when these emotions start to dictate our lives.

"No, I don't want to study, I don't feel good." "I don't want to meet friends, I feel weird today." Over time, this begins to harm our daily life.

I talk to so many students who are taking anxiety pills, feeling depressed, and often finding heavy emotional challenges causing daily trouble.

Is there a solution to this? Yes, indeed, there is, and it's quite similar to overcoming the problem of overthinking: truly understanding what emotions are.

First, understand that emotions are temporary. They don't last forever. They fade quickly if you don't give them attention, and they linger if you give them importance. In both cases, they don't last forever, and that's a relief!

Next, realise that emotions are not always real. They don't always reflect reality. Maybe you're feeling insecure, but in reality, there is no real threat. Perhaps you're feeling sad, but life is going well. This realisation - that emotions are not always real, detaches you from them and allows you to observe them from a distance, instead of identifying with them. It's a deeper way of looking at things.

I personally do this to handle emotions. I consider emotions to be like trains, and myself as a person sitting on a railway station bench. Every now and then, a train full of emotions arrives, inviting me to board. It's my choice whether to get on or let it pass by.

If I choose to board the train, I feel everything that train carries - all the emotions. But if I simply sit and observe the train coming and leaving, I feel relieved.

The best way to handle emotions is to let the train come, stand for a while, make you a bit uncomfortable and then leave you with peace.

You should only be an observer, not a participant.

When the train leaves, you can calmly analyse why it came, why it invited you, and find the cause behind it. This way, you can also find a solution to prevent it from coming back.

I encourage you to read this again. It's deep and important.

"We are not our emotions, but the awareness that observes them. True peace arises when we cease to identify with the waves of feeling and instead learn to navigate them with understanding and stillness."

Sacred Place

We are not the storm we feel,
But the quiet mind, so real.
Emotions rise, like waves they crash,
Yet we, the watcher, remain intact.

True peace is found when we release,
The need to grasp, to fight, to cease.
In stillness, we learn to navigate,
And let the currents dissipate.

Not bound by waves, we sail with grace,
The calm within, our sacred place.

Competition

Imagine you're running a 50 km race. You're exhausted, your heart feels like it's about to burst, but you're almost there. Suddenly, four other runners appear beside you. They're just as determined, and the competition begins. All five of you push yourselves beyond your limits, trying to outrun one another. You're drained, but you keep going because you think there's only one winner.

Now, you're just 100 metres from the finish line. And then, something unexpected happens. You all stop in disbelief. There isn't a single finish line. Instead, each of you has a separate finish line, marked individually.

All of you were meant to win, in your own time, in your own way.

Even if you had taken twice the time, even if you had walked instead of run, you still would have won. Because the race was never about beating others. It was about reaching your own end.

This is life. And sadly, most of us realise this too late.

There is no competition. There is enough space, enough success, enough peace for each one of us.

Competition only exists when the players are the same, but are our lives truly the same? Do we face the same struggles, feel joy in the same things, live under identical circumstances? Not at all. Even two people in the same family live completely different lives.

Competition is a myth, one that society handed down to us. But you don't have to carry it anymore.

Yes, when you're preparing for an exam or running a school race, competition does exist. But ask yourself - *does that competition really define your life?*

If someone else wins the race, does it ruin your future? Does it take away every opportunity meant for you? You already know the answer - it doesn't.

I'm not saying don't compete. Compete, but don't forget to live while doing so. Because in the long run, we all receive what we truly deserve. No one can take that away from you.

Life has enough space, enough success, and enough light for each one of us.

"Compete, but don't forget to live because in the end, life isn't about beating others, it's about becoming who you were meant to be."

Addiction

Addiction is something most teenagers suffer from. For some, it's mobile addiction; for others, it's porn, gaming, tobacco, or something else. I know you try really hard to get rid of these addictions, but now they've become a part of your routine, so deeply rooted that it feels like they can't be removed.

But let me tell you this: it's absolutely possible to get rid of such habits, just not in the way you might think.

Most people, when trying to overcome addictions or bad habits, do what everyone else does, they try to avoid them. To reduce mobile use, they set screen limits. To fight porn addiction, they block websites. This goes on for days - sometimes you win, but eventually, you fall back into the same old patterns.

It's like setting a motivational wallpaper - it works for a while, but soon, you don't even notice it when unlocking your phone.

The real solution requires deeper understanding.

We humans have limited time on Earth, right? Just 24 hours a day. You may think you're addicted to your phone, but in reality, you're just free with no direction. You lack PURPOSE. You simply have enough time to waste on these things.

Understand this through your own life:

When you spend hours on your phone, do you really feel the urge to study? Maybe you feel guilty about not studying, but the urge to study? No, because in your mind, the phone has become the priority.

Now think of a positive example: Do you feel like playing a game one hour before an important exam? No, you just want more time to revise. Because in that moment, scoring well becomes your top priority.

That's the point.

The priorities you set in your mind determine whether you indulge in something useful or wasteful.

Now comes the question: **how do you set your priorities?**
In my opinion, it requires three key elements:

1. **A big aim** — a goal so powerful and meaningful that it ignites a fire within you, strong enough to keep you from wasting your time.

2. **The value of time** — something I'll cover in the upcoming pages.

3. **Self-control** — which I'll also explore later.

When you combine a burning desire (your aim), the value of time, and self-control, something amazing happens - you become *unshakable*. Slowly but surely, bad habits start getting replaced by better ones.

Remember: **you can't keep a garden empty.**

Either the weeds of addiction will take over, or you take charge as the gardener and plant the roses of purpose, growth, and a better life.

Time

We all know that time is valuable, yet we waste it every day.

But why?

The answer is simple: **we humans are terrible at calculation.**

We know time matters, but we don't feel how much it does, not until we see the real numbers in front of us.

So, get ready for a reality check.

Let's say you're 20 years old.
From now on, you decide to use your phone for just 4 hours a day (which, honestly, is less than what most people use).

You stick to this habit for the next 40 years, until you're 60.
Sounds pretty normal, right?

But have you ever done the maths?

- 4 hours/day

- 365 days/year

- 40 years

That's **58,400 hours.**

Now here's the shocker:

58,400 hours = 2,433 days = **6.7 years**

Yes, nearly **7 years** of your life gone.

Not 7 weeks. Not 7 months. **7 entire years**, spent just staring at a screen.

Makes you think, doesn't it?

You know what never comes back? **Time.**

The people you have around you, the life you're living right now - your school days, college life, every single moment you experience - **none of it will return**.

What usually does come back, though, is *regret*.

The regret of not living fully, not enjoying the moment, not using time wisely. The regret that whispers, *"I wish I had lived more... cherished more... made better use of my time."*

"The best time to start was five years ago. The second-best time is NOW."

Self Control

Let me tell you why we love **junk food and experience lust and anger.**

These urges aren't just random, these instincts are hardwired in our biology, and they all have a purpose for our survival.

Junk Food

We crave junk food because our ancestors needed high-calorie foods to survive. Our brains still seek out these foods today, as they release dopamine, the "feel-good" chemical. Unfortunately, junk food is everywhere, and it's designed to keep us hooked.

Lust and Attraction

Lust is our natural drive to reproduce. It's tied to hormones like testosterone and estrogen, which push us to seek out mates and pass on our genes. While it's important for reproduction, modern life can sometimes make us feel lust more than needed.

Anger

Anger is part of our fight or flight response. It helps us protect ourselves or others from danger. In social settings, anger can help set boundaries, but today, it's often triggered by less serious situations, leading to emotional outbursts.

In short, junk food, lust, and anger are biological instincts designed for survival, but they don't always fit in with modern life.

This concept can also apply to many other things.

But why am I telling you this in a topic called "Self-Control"?

It's because when we become aware of why our body behaves the way it does, we understand that not everything we feel requires action. Sometimes, it's unnecessary to act on certain impulses. This is where self-control comes into play.

For example, you might see an attractive man or woman on the road, and your body experiences strange waves of attraction. A typical reaction might be to keep staring or even objectifying the person. But this is where self-control is crucial. Instead of staring at the person like a wild animal, you can simply remind yourself, *"I know where this is coming from, it's just evolutionary instinct. It's nothing to act on."* Then, you can shift your focus back to your work, and the urge will pass.

Another example: You see a cheesy pizza, and you feel like eating it all by yourself. But you think, *"I know this is junk food, and I won't sacrifice my health for a momentary pleasure."*

Getting the point? Self-control, paired with self-awareness, is one of the greatest strengths you can develop.

Self Awareness

The one thing I give most of my time to is self-awareness. In my opinion, there is nothing more important than being self-aware.

You know what? You're breathing. Yes, right now - you're breathing.

And now that I've pointed it out, you probably feel a little uncomfortable or irritated that someone made you aware of something so automatic. Isn't that strange? Breathing is the one thing we can't live without, yet we're rarely conscious of it. And the moment we become aware of it; it feels weird.

Now ask yourself:
Are you aware of your thoughts? Your emotions?
Are you aware of the actions you take daily, and where they're leading you?
Are you aware of how you speak to people?
Of your insecurities and your strengths?
Are you truly aware?
Would you be able to write a book about yourself?

If your answer is "yes," then congratulations. But if not, then you need to become self-aware.

How to become self-aware?

The first step is introspection. Whenever you get the time, reflect on your life, your past, without any bias. Just observe it. This will help you understand yourself better.

The second step is understanding the value of the *present*. The present is all you've truly got. Stop worrying about the future, it will become the present one day. Stop worrying about the past, it's already gone.

"Stop worrying about the future, your future self will handle it, just like your past self survived everything you once thought you couldn't."

Toxicity

Many of us are surrounded by toxic people, but we lack the courage to say goodbye. As "good" humans, we think it might hurt them. But you know what? This isn't a trait of a good human, it's a trait of a foolish one. Let me explain.

Suppose you are a rose. You have the capacity to spread your fragrance far and wide. But every day, someone comes and plucks you, and your fragrance fades within hours. Yet you do nothing, because you're a "nice" person, you don't want to hurt anyone. Really?

Your fragrance could have reached a hundred people, but now it's limited to just one. Is that what being a nice human means?

Understand this deeply: **there's a big difference between being a good person and being an emotional fool.**

Don't be a fool, be a *phool* (flower) instead. Don't let toxicity ruin your true essence. Let yourself evolve like a flower. A flower doesn't force its fragrance, it flows naturally when it stays connected to its roots.

The day you say goodbye to toxicity is the day you'll be truly free. And don't overthink it, you're not doing anything wrong.

You're doing what's right.
Besides, ask yourself honestly: would they cry before leaving you?

Now comes the question: *How do you figure out if someone is toxic?*

Sometimes, the answer is obvious, you just know. But if you find yourself in doubt, here's a powerful way to gain clarity - something I read a long time ago.

Imagine that the person is completely silent, unable to speak. The only way left to judge them is through their actions. And remember, actions always speak louder than words.

Set aside your memories, emotions, and attachments for a moment. Just observe their behaviour. Their actions will give you the answer you're looking for.

But what if the toxicity comes from your family, and you can't leave them? You are forced to live in that environment. In such cases, the solution is twofold: First, acknowledge that you are living in a toxic environment, and understand that not everything said or done is meant to affect you.

Don't let it leave a mark on your sensitive heart - listen, but let it pass through one ear and out the other. Secondly, focus on building your skills and working hard to become independent.

Strive to stand on your own two feet, and one day, when you have the means, you will be able to create your own environment - a peaceful, thriving space where you can flourish. Good luck!

"It is okay to feel sad after making a right decision."

Decision Making

After class 10th, the one thing you do on a regular basis is decision-making.

Which stream should I select in 11th? Which subjects should I opt for? Which exams should I give? Which college should I go to? Which skills should I develop? The list goes on.

In the 21st century, where we have so many choices, decision-making has become a tough and exhausting mental task.

And trust me when I say, I am that person who can never make a decision. I struggle a lot with it; I struggle so much that most of the time, my head starts to hurt. But you know what? I've started to deal with it. Let me explain how.

Over time, I've realised that if a decision isn't harmful - like simply choosing a college or a course, then there's no such thing as a perfect decision. You can never predict the future and what's going to happen.

Saying "yes" to something is saying "no" to something else. In simple terms, if you choose College A, you will never experience College B, C, or D. The problem arises when we start comparing ourselves to others. We look at a student and think, *"Oh, they're so happy at College B; I wish I had gone there instead of College A."* But the reality is, there's a high probability that the student at College B might be thinking the same thing.

To be honest, happiness isn't a destination; it's a mindset. When you go to college, you'll notice some students hating their college experience while others love it. And trust me, I've spoken to many students, and I've seen this in the topmost colleges. I've seen all-India toppers crying, while students who didn't rank as high are enjoying their time. Experiences are so subjective.

So, the first step is realising that we can never predict the outcome of the decisions we make, in most cases.

When making a decision, make sure it isn't harmful. For example, choosing whether to go to college or take a gap year is a serious decision, you need to carefully consider what feels right for you.

But when it comes to decisions where there's no real "right or wrong," like whether to develop singing skills or dancing skills, just do what makes you happy. You never know if singing will lead to success, or dancing will, or maybe both, or neither.

That's something only the future can reveal, so why worry now?

Through this, I've realised that there are mainly two reasons we hesitate to make decisions. First is the **fear of the unknown**, the anxiety about what the future holds, especially when you're stepping into something unfamiliar and uncertain. The second is **uncertainty**, the doubt that even though something feels right in your mind, it might turn out to be wrong in reality.

The best way to deal with this is to take a pen and notebook, and write a big **"WHY"** in the middle of the page. Ask yourself: *"Why am I taking this decision?"*

Then start writing down everything that comes to your mind, why you want to do it, why you're afraid, what draws your interest, what research you've done, what you still need to do, and so on. Pour it all out.

Slowly, you'll notice your fear starts to fade. Because now, you're not making a decision on a whim, you're making it after reflection and research. So, no matter what the future holds, you won't live with regret.

You'll know that you made the decision with awareness, not ignorance.

"Awareness is not the absence of doubt, but the presence of understanding - while ignorance walks blindly, convinced it sees."

Pro Tip: Whenever possible, take quick action. Thoughts alone won't take you anywhere, but actions will. If I had only kept thinking, I would've never written this book. **Act as fast as you can**, let the details and problems figure themselves out later.

"Some people chase happiness all their lives, not realising they once held it in a fleeting, ordinary moment they didn't know to cherish."

The Art of Saying No!

Many of us face this problem, right?
Saying "no" feels almost impossible. We often think it's a bad thing, that it might hurt someone's feelings or make things awkward. But here's the real issue: in the race to avoid saying "no," we end up sacrificing our own time.

We aren't always free. We have our own responsibilities, our own work. But because we struggle with saying "no," we constantly put ourselves last.

So, **how can you say no without guilt?**
Let me share two simple strategies:

1. Ask for permission to say no.
Instead of directly refusing, ask for permission. Try saying something like, *"Would it be okay if I say no? I hope you won't mind."*

Trust me, this works more often than you'd expect.

For example, if a friend asks you for a favour and you can't help, just say, *"Will it be alright if I say no? I really hope you understand."* Most of the time, people respond with, *"It's okay, no problem."*

2. Flip the situation.
Imagine this: you ask someone for a favour, and they reply politely, *"I'm really sorry, I'm busy right now. I wish I could help, but I can't."*

Would you feel deeply hurt? Probably not. You might feel a little disappointed, but you'd understand, they're just busy.

Now apply that same logic to yourself.

If you say "no" politely, the right people will understand. And if they don't, it's not your fault. That's their fragile ego speaking, not a failure on your part.

In fact, people who can't respect a simple "no" probably didn't deserve your help in the first place.

Anxiety

Who loves anxiety?
That strange, heavy feeling that's hard to even describe. It creeps in quietly, making life feel dull, empty, sometimes even meaningless.

But have you noticed?
Some people seem genuinely happier, not because their lives are perfect, but because they don't let anxiety control them.
How do they do it?

Thoughts, overthinking, and overwhelming emotions play a huge role in anxiety. If you learn to handle these, half the battle is already won, and I've spoken about this in depth before.

But let's now talk about what else can help.

One of the most powerful ways to deal with anxiety is to ask yourself this simple question: *"What's the best that can happen and what's the worst?"*

Take the fear of failure, for instance.
The best that can happen? You succeed. Which means your anxiety was just noise. The worst? **You fail!**

Now pause and truly think:
If you fail, will your life be over? No.
Will you never get another chance? No.
Will you survive it and grow stronger? Absolutely yes.

You've done it before, turned failures into stepping stones. You've bounced back even when you thought you wouldn't. And slowly, as this truth sinks in, you'll realise*: "Even if the worst happens, I can handle it."*

And that realisation?
It starts to melt anxiety away.

Sometimes, anxiety arises simply because we lack clarity.
We're unsure about something, and that uncertainty starts to eat us from within.

One of the most effective ways to deal with this kind of anxiety is through **clear communication**.

If a friend is the source of your anxiety, talk to them.
Express what you're feeling - honestly, calmly, and openly.

Most of the time, you'll notice something beautiful:
Just the act of expressing yourself brings relief.

Even before the problem is solved, your mind feels lighter.
Because anxiety often isn't about what's happening, it's about what's left unsaid.

Now comes another question:

What should you do when you're under heavy anxiety?

Let's be honest, telling someone to "just relax" during an anxiety attack is like asking a wall to move. It doesn't work. So, what can we actually do?

I'm not a psychologist, but I'll share what **works for me**.

Step one: Recognise anxiety as anxiety.

Think about it.
When you catch a cold: your nose runs, your body shivers, you get a headache, yet you simply say, *"I have a cold."*
But we don't treat anxiety the same way.

When anxiety strikes, we panic:
"My heart is racing."
"I'm sweating."
"My vision is blurring, should I rush to the hospital?"

We treat each symptom like a separate emergency. But in truth, it's all part of **anxiety**.

Once you accept that, the symptoms lose some of their power. You stop fearing every sensation, and that alone brings a kind of calm.

Step two: Use the 5-4-3-2-1 Grounding Technique.

When you feel overwhelmed, try this:

1. **5 things you can see** – Look around and name five things. Notice the colours, shapes, or textures.

2. **4 things you can touch** – Your clothes, a table, the floor, anything physical.

3. **3 things you can hear** – A bird, the fan, your own breath.

4. **2 things you can smell** – Maybe your soap, food nearby, or even the air.

5. **1 thing you can taste** – It could be gum, a drink, or just the natural taste in your mouth.

You've probably seen this on social media, but **trust me, it works.** It gently pulls your mind back to the present.

Final step: Let it come, and let it go.

The more you try to fight anxiety, the more power you give it.

But the more you observe it, just watch it come and go like a wave, the smaller it becomes.

This step does require a deeper understanding of your thoughts and emotions, which I've already discussed earlier in this book. But once you get there, you'll find that anxiety doesn't have to control your life.

"When the Storm Comes"

When the storm of thoughts begins to rise,
And panic dances behind your eyes,
Pause, dear soul, and take a breath,
It's not the end, it's not your death.

Your heart may race, your hands may shake,
But this is not a sign to break.
Name what you see, what you feel, what's near,
Ground yourself, there's nothing to fear.

Let the wave pass, don't swim upstream,
You're not your thoughts, nor every dream.
In stillness, strength will softly grow,
Let it come, and let it go.

Morality

Morality is the belief system that helps us distinguish between right and wrong, guiding us to make choices that are good, fair, and just. But the problem with morality is that it's highly subjective.

Consider the act of lying. In some situations, people may believe that lying to protect someone's feelings is morally right, while in others, honesty is seen as the higher moral ground, even if it causes temporary discomfort.

For example, telling a friend that their outfit doesn't look good might feel harsh, but necessary for honesty. On the other hand, someone else might think it's kinder to spare their feelings. This shows how moral views can shift based on the situation and perspective.

The real struggle begins when these moral dilemmas start interfering with your daily life. You begin overthinking every single action, wondering, *is it right or wrong?* - and that can feel overwhelming.

I've faced this too, and even today, I still do. The more people you interact with, the more confusing it gets. *What should I do? What should I not do? Will this be morally right or will I end up hurting someone?*

But I've found a solution that works for me, and I hope it helps you too.

Whenever I take a decision or perform an action, I simply ask myself: **"If someone did the same to me, with the same intention and mindset, and I fully understood it - would it hurt me?"**

If the answer is no, I go ahead without hesitation.

Let me give you a small, silly example.

I hate lying. But sometimes when a student messages me saying, *"Is it possible to complete the syllabus in one week? I've done nothing and I'm terrified,"*

What do I say? I reply, *"Yes, just work hard - anything is possible."*

In reality, I know one week isn't enough. But if I say that bluntly, the student might lose all motivation. That small hope - *"yes, it's possible"*, can give them the push to do their best.

- My action – telling a lie

- My intention – to boost the student's morale

- Would I feel bad if someone did the same for me and I understood their intention? – Not at all. I'd actually feel thankful they didn't crush my hope, but instead encouraged me.

Is lying morally right? – Absolutely not.
Is lying right in this situation? **– Absolutely yes.**

Imagine a mother telling her hungry child that food is on the way, even when she has nothing to offer yet, just to keep the child hopeful and calm.

Technically, she's lying. But is it morally wrong?

Her intention is to protect her child's emotional well-being, to avoid panic or despair. From the outside, it's a lie. But from the inside, it's an act of love.

This is where morality becomes less about rules and more about reasons.

Fear

We all have fears, right? Some have common fears which everyone has like fear of the stage or lizards while some have less common fears, like the fear of meeting people.

Some fears occur rarely, like stage fear (since most people don't speak on stage daily), but others like the fear of going out, fear of traffic, or fear of people judging you can literally harm your day-to-day life.

I always had fears that were uncommon, but they happened to me very often. A scary mix, right? Meeting your fears daily!

In the year 2023, I fell severely ill. A small stomach infection turned into something really big. Every single day became a living hell. And to be honest, even today, while writing this, I'm still suffering - I haven't healed completely.

When I got severely ill, one big problem I faced was developing new fears. I stopped talking to people. I stopped attending calls. I stopped going outside.

I don't know how to explain this exactly, but maybe this will help you understand: suppose you pick up a call one day and hear shocking news. How do you feel the next day when the phone rings again? You feel anxious, right? Maybe for the whole month. That's how the body works.

So, me having so many symptoms and suffering led me into this trap of fear.

It started ruining my life, and I had to deal with it. Slowly, I realised that life waits for no one. Whether you laugh, cry, sit, or walk - life goes on. But fear stays the same if you let it.

I started facing my fears - even when they scared me. Just like picking up the phone even when the ring causes anxiety.

Surprisingly, I survived the fears. They were not as big as I had shaped them in my mind.

I learned my lessons. First, things are sometimes not as big as we think they are. Second, **the only way to stop facing fears again and again is to face them regularly.**

"The only thing we have to fear is fear itself."

— Franklin D. Roosevelt

The Heart Behind the Act

In shadows grey, not black or white,
We search for what is just and right.
Not every truth is loud and clear,
Some wear the mask of love or fear.
The act may seem a little wrong,
But if the heart is beating strong,
Then kindness hides in every choice,
And silent morals find their voice.

Language

I would like to end this section by talking about something most people overlook - **language**.

You might wonder, *"What does language have to do with mental health?"* But trust me when I say, **language is of utmost importance**.

Think about it: when you say *"I exist"*, *"I am happy"*, or even *"I am anxious"*, you're using language.

The very idea of the ego - the ***"I"*** - is shaped by a single letter.

Most people cannot even think without language; there's a constant **inner monologue** running in their heads.

Yet, ironically, language is what we pay the **least** attention to.

Have you ever noticed how people talk these days?
How often do you hear someone abuse in a single sentence?

Honestly, it's not rare to hear 1–3 abusive words in every line. It's become so common that even casual conversations end with disrespect.

And please, don't say that *abusing helps release anger*.

That's a **third-class excuse**, not a solution.
There are countless ways to deal with anger.
So why choose the worst one?

And what do most people consume on social media?
Let's be honest, we both know it's mostly trash.
But how many of us **consciously** choose to avoid it? Very few.

Now think about this: You spend your entire day speaking harshly, watching negativity, listening to drama and then expect your mind to be peaceful and healthy?

That's not just strange, it's unfair to yourself.

Believe it or not, I've never used foul language - I don't curse or abuse. I avoid trash content. I speak to people with respect.
Because for me, **language is sacred**.

And honestly, it doesn't take an "intellectual" to realise the importance of language. It just takes awareness.

There are countless topics I could dive into in this section, but I'm only focusing on what I truly believe will serve you in this book.

Some of these other ideas might find their place on another day, or maybe in a future book. For now, I'll put my pen down here, wrapping up this topic with the hope that it adds real value to your journey.

"Language is not just a tool of communication; it's the mirror of the mind. What you speak, you become."

"Every abusive word spoken isn't just sound, it's a seed planted in your mind. Choose wisely."

8. Productive Mindset

*"True productivity isn't about doing more, it's about doing what matters
with intention."*

-   Unknown

Why Productivity?

Some time ago, I asked a highly productive man, *"Sir, why are you so
productive and time-conscious? Don't you ever feel like going off-
schedule or procrastinating a bit?"*

His reply was unexpectedly profound.

He said, *"I love productivity because it works for me."*
Do you get that? He didn't just force himself to be productive, he
embraced it because, in the long run, it made his life better. He's ahead
of many people, he earns well, lives well, stays healthy, and much more.

But here's the interesting point: if this is true, then the opposite is also true.
In the long run, if you're not productive or time-conscious, those habits
will slowly eat away at your life and ruin it.

I hope this simple, straightforward motivation is enough to begin this
section, where I'll be sharing almost everything I know about productivity.

We Cannot Sit Quiet

Most of us humans don't have the ability to sit quietly and do nothing, we
constantly feel the need to stay engaged.

Just look around your locality: you'll see everyone doing something. An
unemployed person might be sitting somewhere chatting and wasting time,
an elderly person may be enjoying conversations with friends, and so on.

You rarely see anyone doing **absolutely nothing**. That's a skill only a few can master.

So, if we can't sit idle, why not use this restlessness for our own benefit?

But instead, what do we usually do? We doomscroll on Instagram, talk to friends about meaningless things, binge-watch games or shows on TV or our phones, and so much more.

As I mentioned earlier in the topic of habits and addiction, when we don't have a clear **PURPOSE**, we naturally drift towards useless activities and end up wasting time. But the moment we have a ***burning desire***, everything changes. Whenever we feel a strong urge to do something, we choose something productive, not something pointless.

So, use your restlessness to your advantage. Have a clear purpose or goal to achieve, and be mentally prepared for it. You'll automatically drift away from time-wasting habits and move towards something meaningful.

"Restlessness is not your enemy - it's your energy asking for direction. Give it a purpose, and it will build your future instead of wasting your present."

Five Years

You're playing a game or watching a movie. Your parents scold you for it, but instead of stopping, you feel irritated, you feel like your freedom is being taken away. So you continue. Only later do you realise they were right. You just wasted precious time.

But the problem with this realisation is, it always comes after the time is already gone.

There's one simple habit that can save you from falling into this trap: **Ask yourself before doing anything - *"Will this matter in 5 years? Will it make any sense then?"***

For example, learning a skill probably will. Watching a random movie? Probably not.

When I was in 9th grade, I downloaded a game on my phone called *Clash of Clans*. It was addictive and demanded hours and hours of investment. Being young, I gave in. I wasted months on it.

But one day, I had a shocking realisation: all that effort only mattered inside the game. In the real world, it meant **nothing**. That moment changed me. Since that day, you'll rarely find games on my phone, and I rarely watch movies either.

Why waste the limited time we have on Earth on things that won't matter after a while?

Eisenhower Matrix

There are so many tasks we handle in our daily lives, and at times, it can become overwhelming. Sometimes, we notice that less important tasks consume so much of our time that we're left with little for what truly matters. And at other times, we aren't even aware of this until it's too late. This is where the Eisenhower Matrix comes in.

The **Eisenhower Matrix** named after U.S. President Dwight D. Eisenhower, offers a simple but profound way to categorise and prioritise your tasks.

By focusing on what truly matters, we can manage our time more effectively and avoid wasting precious moments on the less important things.

The matrix divides tasks into four quadrants, based on their **urgency** and **importance**:

1. Important and Urgent (Do Now)

These are the tasks that need immediate action. They are both significant and time-sensitive. For example, preparing for a surprise test or resolving an urgent issue with a class project. These tasks cannot be delayed and should be tackled immediately to prevent negative consequences.

2. Important but Not Urgent (Plan and Schedule)

These tasks are the **real gold** for your success. They may not scream for your immediate attention, but they are the ones that will shape your long-term achievements.

For instance, regular studying, sleeping, exercising, and maintaining relationships all fall into this category. These actions may seem less urgent in the moment, but they are essential for your personal growth and well-being.

By consistently working on these tasks, you are laying a strong foundation for the future, and that is what truly drives success. The key here is consistency. You may not feel the immediate rewards, but in time, these investments will pay off significantly.

3. Not Important but Urgent (Delegate if Possible)

These are tasks that require quick attention but don't significantly contribute to your long-term success. For instance, responding to an email that doesn't have much relevance to your immediate goals or dealing with a minor problem in your daily routine. If possible, delegate these tasks to others or complete them quickly without letting them consume too much of your energy.

4. Not Important and Not Urgent (Eliminate or Delay)

These are the distractions, activities that don't contribute to your growth and can be delayed indefinitely. For example, mindlessly scrolling through social media or watching random videos. These tasks can be eliminated or postponed to free up your time for more meaningful activities.

The Role of Time in Prioritisation

While the Eisenhower Matrix is powerful, one additional factor we should consider is **time**. Some tasks, though they may fall into the "Not Important and Not Urgent" category, may take very little time.

For example, making a quick phone call to a friend or responding to a short message. These tasks can often be handled immediately, as they only require a few minutes and don't significantly disrupt your schedule.

On the other hand, some tasks that are **Important but Not Urgent** might take longer to complete. These should be scheduled, but don't feel pressured to finish them immediately. Breaking them into smaller, manageable steps can make them easier to tackle over time.

By incorporating the **time** factor into your decision-making, you can further fine-tune your approach to productivity.

I personally apply the concept of importance, urgency, and time, and it has greatly helped me become more productive.

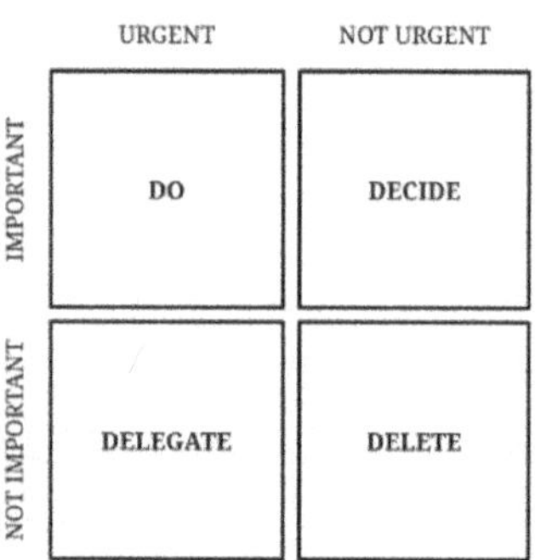

A Day Before

One thing that really helps me, and many others, is making a rough plan a night before for what we're going to do the next day.

As I'm writing this, I can tell you that last night, I decided I would write this today, and here I am doing it. Planning is crucial.

Waking up in the morning without any clear direction can leave you feeling lost, but when you wake up with a purpose or a rough plan in mind, it's much easier to stay productive throughout the day.

It's simple to follow - just before going to sleep, take a moment to think about or write down your main goals for tomorrow. And if you miss that step, make sure to do it first thing after waking up.

"Your day begins the moment you decide how it will unfold; planning isn't just about tasks; it's about shaping your purpose and setting the course for success."

Emotional Stability

I've noticed several times that when my day turns unproductive, there are always common factors at play.

It could be that my day didn't start well, my sleep schedule got disrupted, I spoke to someone who emotionally drained me, or something negatively impacted my focus or work.

In short, **anything that occupies your mind** can become a barrier to productivity, so it's crucial to stay away from such distractions.

Sometimes, these things are beyond our control, and that's okay. However, we still have the power to choose how we react. More often than not, though, these factors are within our ability to manage.

Pay attention to the common elements that lead to unproductive days, whether it's a web series that pulls you in, a friend who drains your energy, or something else, and either remove or manage it from your life as soon as possible.

Routine

The majority of students don't follow a routine, they don't have a fixed time to sleep or wake up, no set time to eat, and no structure to their day.

I completely understand that being a student isn't easy, and following a strict routine can be challenging. But even then, having some form of routine is important, even if it's not perfectly fixed.

A routine matters for many reasons. First, it helps you track your life over the long run. It keeps your energy levels balanced and your mood stable. Most importantly, it naturally makes you more productive, because having a routine means you're doing things with awareness and intention.

There's no "ideal" routine, whatever works for you, works for you. But do make an effort to create one. Sleeping at 3 a.m. from Monday to Saturday and then sleeping all day on Sundays and holidays won't lead you anywhere meaningful. Please understand this.

Sleep

It is scientifically proven that quality sleep is one of the biggest factors in living a healthy and productive life.

Aim for at least 6 hours of sleep a day, ideally 8, because sleep is crucial.

When we sleep well, our brain gets a chance to recharge and reset. During the deeper stages of sleep, especially REM sleep [Rapid Eye Movement sleep is a deep stage of sleep where most dreaming occurs, and it's crucial for emotional processing, memory consolidation, and overall brain restoration.], it consolidates memory, clears mental fog, and processes emotions. That's why after a proper night's rest, we think more clearly, solve problems faster, and make better decisions.

Personally, I've observed a clear difference: on days I'm well-rested, I get more done in less time and feel emotionally steady. I'm less irritable, more focused, and even the smallest tasks don't feel like a burden. On the other hand, sleep deprivation slows everything down - my concentration drops,

I procrastinate more, and even things I normally enjoy begin to feel draining.

So if there's one habit I recommend you protect above all, it's your sleep schedule. Good sleep isn't a luxury, it's the foundation of a productive and peaceful life.

No matter what's going on in my life, I never sacrifice my sleep.

Delayed Gratification

One thing most people don't realise is that the most important things in life rarely give us immediate pleasure or happiness. They take time, sometimes a long time, before we start seeing results or feeling their true value.

For example, studying for exams won't make you a topper overnight; it may take years. Going to the gym won't make you healthy in a day, and eating clean won't show visible results instantly. Anything truly valuable requires consistency and patience.

On the other hand, almost everything that gives instant pleasure often lacks long-term value - scrolling on social media, smoking, or any kind of addiction gives immediate satisfaction, but adds no real meaning to your life.

The person who truly understands this difference, between instant gratification and long-term growth, becomes highly productive. Trust me.

Don't Speak

You wish to become the topper of your school. Just the thought of it fills you with excitement.

What do you do next? You rush to tell your friends, *"I'm working really hard to become the topper! Once I achieve it, I'll do this, I'll do that…"*

But trust me, don't do this. There's a logical reason behind it.

As humans, we have a natural tendency to express our excitement. That's why we click so many pictures while doing something great, to post them on social media. We love to share our aspirations.

However, here's the problem: our mind gets confused.

When you feel excited about a goal, like becoming a topper, your brain starts craving that excitement and uses it as motivation to push you forward.

But the moment you talk about your goal too much, before actually achieving it, your brain experiences that same sense of reward as if you've already succeeded.

And if your mind can feel the pleasure of achievement just by expressing it, why would it still work hard to earn it?

You may have noticed this yourself: something that once excited you deeply becomes less exciting once you've told many people about it.

So, hold that feeling in. Let the pressure of not expressing it build up. Channel it into your work. And one day, your actions will speak louder than any words, and the pleasure you feel then will be real, earned, and long-lasting.

Psychologically, it's backed by research too - when we talk about our goals, especially in great detail, our brain releases dopamine, the same "reward" chemical we get from actually achieving the goal.

This premature sense of accomplishment can reduce our drive to follow through. This is known as **"social reality substitution."**

Trust the Nudge

Somehow, our mind already knows what's right for us. You may have noticed this too, let me explain how.

You don't force it, but your mind naturally gives you a gentle nudge about what the right thing to do is in that moment.

For instance, just when vacations start, your first thought might be, *"I should finish my homework now so I won't struggle later,"* or *"I should study before watching a movie."* But we often ignore these thoughts, telling ourselves, *"I'll do it later."*

A small change in your habit can shift everything. Instead of ignoring that first thought, start giving it importance.

Suppose you're about to open your phone and a thought comes - *"I should revise first."* Instead of brushing it aside, pause for a second and ask yourself: *"Is this thought worth acting on?"* If the answer is yes, don't let your mind negotiate by saying things like, *"I'll do it after this or that."* Just act immediately, if possible.

Negotiation

You decide to wake up early in the morning. You set an alarm, feeling highly motivated, and go to sleep. But when the alarm actually rings, it feels like your entire personality changes, you no longer want to wake up. All you crave is more sleep. You start to give up, and before you know it, you fall back asleep. Later, when you finally wake up, your entire mood is ruined.

One thing is common every time this happens: **negotiation**. Our mind doesn't simply quit, it craves a valid excuse before giving in.

So instead of just snoozing the alarm, it starts making a deal. It says, *"Yesterday was tiring, and I slept late. I know I wanted to wake up early, but if I do, I'll be low on energy all day. Waking up two hours later won't really make a difference."* And once the mind convinces itself with this reasoning, it acts.

Don't fall into this trap. Don't let your mind begin that negotiation. The only way to win is to act on your intention before it turns into a debate.

Get up as soon as the thought comes, before your mind starts negotiating.

"The moment you hesitate, the mind negotiates. Act before it starts to speak."

Do The Right

By now, you must have realised that the mind is full of **duality**. It rarely sticks to one thing.

At night, it promises to wake up early; in the morning, it begs for more sleep. And once it gets that extra sleep, it regrets not waking up. The same mind that's addicted says, *"I need to quit this addiction."* The same mind that gets angry says, *"I shouldn't have been angry."*

Your mind is both the problem and the cure.

Once you truly understand this, you'll see that blindly following your mind isn't always wise. Instead, act based on what's right. Don't let the mind control you, you must take control of your mind.

Whenever your mind says something, pause and ask: *"Is this right or wrong?"* Only act if the answer is **right**. And when you're completely confused, let the mind chatter in the background, but go ahead and do what you know is right.

In the morning, when you wake up, the right choice is to get up and chase your goals. That simple realisation of ***what's right*** is enough to take action.

Do what is right - all the time.

The Mind Speaks

The mind speaks in echoes, never just one voice,
It tempts with comfort, then mourns the choice.
It's both the cage and the broken key,
Whispers of right drowned in what might be.
At night it dreams, at dawn it hides,
It leads you astray, then shifts to your side.
But truth is quiet - learn to hear it clear,
Act on what's right, not what you fear.

Identity

How do you see yourself? Are you proud of who you are? Do you believe you're capable of achieving the goals you dream about?

The truth is - it all depends on **how you think about yourself**.

Many students don't just fail exams because they didn't study; they fail because they believed they couldn't. And that's deeper than it seems.

The only way to change this is by building a **powerful identity**. And by identity, I mean something so meaningful and vast that even a lifetime wouldn't be enough to fully achieve it.

If you say, *"I want to be a school topper,"* what happens once you become one? The journey ends. You'll only do what's necessary to reach that narrow goal, and nothing more. But if your identity is *"I am a learner,"* can that ever end? Can anyone ever truly learn everything there is to know?

Never. That identity keeps you growing, always.

Don't say, *"I want to finish this book,"* instead say, *"I am a reader."* Don't say, *"I am a negative person,"* say, *"I am a highly positive person in the making."*

Your identity should be **big, positive, and impactful**. Only then will your actions become powerful and focused.

A person who only wants 10 can never reach 100. But a person aiming for 100 will often achieve 10 - **without even trying**.

"Don't build your identity around goals - build it around growth. Goals end, but a strong identity keeps you evolving forever."

Mind Is Not a Dustbin

Have you ever noticed how your mind suddenly starts singing a random song while studying, or how a sad memory pops up right in the middle of an exam? Why can't we just focus on what's important?

The truth is, we treat our mind like a dustbin. We fill it with endless trash - reels, shorts, web series, gossip, meaningless conversations, and then expect it to perform with clarity and perfection.

Think of this: even if a room is filled with the fragrance of roses, just one small piece of dung will ruin the entire smell. That's exactly how the mind works.

For a garden to flourish, you must regularly remove the weeds. Similarly, for the mind to focus, you must remove the distractions.

I'm not saying you should do nothing but study. I'm saying: prioritise what matters, and give minimal time to distractions. And when exams or important goals are near, completely avoid the things you know will hijack your focus. Protect your mind like a sacred space - because it is.

Living In Extremes

One mistake I made for most of my life was living in extremes - either zero or a hundred. But this isn't the best way to live. Living like this only makes you less productive and more stressed.

Let me give you an example. When I was a kid, I used to be quite silly. If I planned to study at 5 AM and woke up at 5:10 instead, I'd just go back to sleep, thinking *"Uff, I missed it. The whole day is ruined."* If I decided to do an assignment and made even a small mistake, my entire mood would be spoiled. I'd waste time correcting silly errors that nobody else would even notice. Perfectionism was never the real problem, the real problem was living in extremes.

I see many students doing the same. They make a timetable and then throw it away just because they missed one day. But over time, I realised this was a big mistake.

Simply understand this - suppose you drink only one glass of water a day. Then someone tells you to drink eight. You agree, but you're only able to drink five. Now, an extremist will feel defeated and go back to drinking just one. But a wise person will say, *"Even five is better than one,"* and try to gradually improve.

That's what I want you to learn: something is always better than nothing. Don't live in extremes. Being a perfectionist is fine, but remember, true perfection comes in the long term. Trying to make one moment perfect can often ruin it. If you notice a mistake, learn from it, improve in the future, but don't get stuck in it.

Will Life Become Boring?

Whenever I talk about productivity, one thing I hear the most is, *"A productive life is a boring life. A normal life is way better than working like a machine."* But this is completely untrue.

Before writing this section on productivity, I introspected a lot because I only wanted to share things that I truly follow myself.

After deep reflection, I also spoke to people who know me well. I asked one of them, *"In your opinion, what are the things I do differently that make me so productive?"* The answer was, *"You were born productive."*

We both laughed, but that answer made me realise something important: **I truly enjoy being productive.**

When you sleep at night with a smile on your face, knowing you've done everything you promised yourself you would do - that feeling is unmatched. Seeing your goals come true because you worked hard for them is a feeling that can't be compared to anything else.

And who says productive people don't enjoy life? They do everything others do, but it becomes a conscious choice. **That's the big difference.**

"Productivity is not merely the act of doing, but the quiet fulfilment in knowing each intentional moment shapes the life you are meant to live, where passion and purpose coexist in harmony."

Is It Hard?

Most people assume that being productive is hard, but the reality is, it's not. It's not even about effort. It's simply a way of living.

Imagine someone who loves eating junk food twice a day. One day, they fall seriously ill and the doctor warns them: *"Stop eating junk, or it could cost you your life."*

What do you think they'll do? Of course, they'll stop, without hesitation. Unless they're mentally unwell, they won't even think twice.

Why? Because now they know, with certainty, the consequences of continuing. Their life literally depends on the choice.

The same applies to productivity. You become truly productive **the day** you realise the consequences of not being productive. And for that, you don't need a doctor, your past is enough.

You still regret not making the right decisions at the right time, don't you? You still feel that if you had been more active in your childhood, you could have been far ahead by now, right? You are completely aware, and yet you choose not to be productive? Why, dear?

Why harm yourself like this, even after knowing the truth?

Don't do this to yourself. Your family has sacrificed so much for you.

You have sacrificed so much for your own future.

Don't let it all go to waste. **You deserve better.**

"True change begins when the weight of today becomes heavier than the weight of the fear of change."

9. Life Lessons and Motivation

"And, when you want something, all the universe conspires in helping you to achieve it."

- *Paulo Coelho, The Alchemist*

Analysis Paralysis?

This might help! There is a term called '**Analysis-Paralysis**', and most of us suffer from it. I'll explain it through an example which you may relate to.

You all will be appearing for exams soon, but most of you have not started preparing yet. Why? The syllabus is tricky, and you don't know which channel to study from, or which books to follow because so many options are available. So, what do you do?

You start analysing. You create a mental image of how you will complete the syllabus, but in the end, you get so overwhelmed that you say, "ahhh, I'll do it tomorrow," but that tomorrow never comes.

This unnecessary analysis, paralyses your actions. It's the same as scrolling through Netflix or YouTube, thinking about which video or movie to watch, and ending up watching nothing. It's just like searching for a good topic for a project and ending up just searching and not selecting any.

Our minds love to create an imaginary world where we are being productive, but in reality, you are just in analysis paralysis. So, stop this analysis game and start with what you have and what you know, and figure out rest of the things in between. I hope it helps!

Usual Way of Being

It's hard to explain, but I'll give it a try.

What we do most often gradually becomes our usual way of being (read twice). For instance, ask any alcohol addict why they drink, and they'll say they feel strange without it. For them, being sober feels strange, but if we have even a sip of alcohol, we might feel overwhelmed because sobriety is our natural state.

- Our natural state: Being Sober
- Their natural state: Being Drunk

 Similarly, the same applies to emotions. If you're always angry, sad, or complaining, those feelings become your normal state, and you don't notice anything unusual about them.

But if you try to change, like avoiding anger for a month or two and then suddenly get angry somehow, you'll feel it more intensely; it won't feel natural anymore. You'll feel the physical and mental toll it takes. Your body will start to reject it, despite it being a natural part of you earlier.

So, don't let bad habits become a part of who you are. The only way to become better is to acknowledge and confront those habits, and it's only possible if they're not a natural part of your life. Otherwise, they'll become your new normal.

I hope that helps clarify things!

Past, Present and Future

Many students message me, expressing feelings of hopelessness, fear, and uncertainty about the future, and suffering from stress and anxiety as exams approach. They feel they have not put in the required hard work, and even if some of them have, they still find the future intimidating.

So, let me tell you something: If I were to ask you to jump from a height of two feet, would you be able to do it? The answer is, of course, yes. Even a five-year-old knows that jumping from a height of two feet is not a big deal.

But now, imagine someone who has created a mental block, believing he or she cannot jump from a height of two feet. Will he or she ever try? You know the answer. If you never try, how will you ever know if you are capable or not? Now, let's twist the story.

Someone becomes too optimistic and jumps from the second floor, breaking his or her legs. This is also wrong: over-optimism.

Now, let's twist the story again. Someone jumps from only two feet, thinking it's easy, but twists his or her leg and breaks it. Now, he or she never tries again because of a bad experience. This is called over-pessimism. One bad accident leads him or her to doubt so many things.

Keep in mind that a blend of pessimistic and optimistic perspectives is essential for success in life. Don't dwell too much on the past or the future. Just take action so you won't regret not trying in the future.

A wise individual smiles at the end, regardless of the outcome, knowing they gave his or her best effort.

The Wisdom of Letting Go

When you become wise, you realise that much of life is beyond your control - the place you are born, the parents you have, the people you meet, the language you first speak, the religion you are introduced to, and so on. So much of who we are is shaped by our environment.

What does this teach us? It teaches us that both success and failure are often part of this larger phenomenon, where we shouldn't take full responsibility for either. Perhaps you succeeded because you were lucky - you had the right mentors, the right opportunities, the right people around you. Or perhaps you failed because circumstances were not in your favour.

This realisation keeps you grounded, preventing ego when you succeed and offering peace when you fail. It also nurtures empathy for others, as you understand that their actions and outcomes are sometimes shaped by forces beyond their control.

Wisdom of Dependent Origination

You do not exist independently. To survive, you need three essential things - oxygen, water, and food. But none of these truly belong to you.

Trees provide oxygen freely, the Earth gives you food, and water comes from nature. Even your very existence depends on others - you are born from someone's body, requiring two genders to unite. Your body grows from the food and water you consume, the mornings you cherish exist because of the sun, and this cycle continues endlessly.

As the Buddha said, ***"When this exists, that exists; when this arises, that arises."*** Everything is interconnected; nothing stands alone.

What does this teach us? That cooperation is always better than competition. The world has enough for all of us, there is no need for jealousy, hatred, or comparison. Love is the only truth. In the end, we are different, yet one.

Be Grateful

We complain so often - I don't like this food; I want that instead. Where is my birthday gift? I need a new, expensive phone. I can't study because I don't have my own room.

We cry over so many things - I failed an exam, my friend isn't talking to me, I don't have a new dress to wear, my trip got cancelled. But do we ever realise how lucky we are?

When you complain about going to school, there's a child who has no school to attend. When you cry for new clothes, there's a boy selling tea, wearing the same shirt for a week. When you complain, a girl somewhere is helping her mother wash clothes in someone else's home. When you reject food, someone else is going to bed hungry.

How can we not appreciate what life has already given us?

Yes, we all strive to make our lives better, but we must never forget, it's already good.

There are people like us, blessed enough to give, and there are others who don't even have the basics, like a blanket to keep warm.

This is reality, not just a story, but life. Let's take a moment to be deeply, genuinely grateful for everything we have. And if we can, let's share a little of that abundance with those who need it most.

23 Lessons from 23 Years [23/01/2024]

Wrapping up my 23rd birthday with 23 lessons from 23 years. Here we go!

1. Whenever a good idea strikes, act on it immediately. Don't let the energy or motivation fade.

2. Take full responsibility for your life, even for things you didn't cause. Responsibility builds courage and resilience.

3. Gratitude is incredibly powerful. Truly feel it - don't just say it. It helps you realise that everything you have is enough, if not more than enough.

4. Slow is fast. Learn patience before life teaches it the hard way. Patience brings calmness.

5. Understand the deference between being a good person and being a fool.

6. Earning respect and trust is one of the hardest things. It requires immense effort, a strong, well-crafted personality, and many sacrifices.

7. Eat good food; trust me, health is wealth. I'll be having moong dal roti on my birthday (chronic infection) because I neglected this, lol. I hope you don't make the same mistake.

8. When faced with a moral dilemma, think about how you'd feel if someone did to you exactly what you're considering doing, fully aware of the intent and purpose. If you'd feel okay with it, you're on the right track.

9. There is no end to learning. Acquire as much knowledge as you can.

10. Our mind will always find a justification for actions rooted in selfish interests. For example, if I get a pan masala sponsorship for ₹10 lakh, my mind might say, *"Do it - your audience is wise and won't buy it anyway,*

and if you don't, someone else will." You see the point? Be aware of such excuses. Don't let them lead you to take the wrong actions. Integrity comes first.

11. I used to feel nostalgic and sad about the past and worried about the future, only to realise that happiness lies in the present. If you are content in the present, neither the future nor the past will scare you much.

12. All it takes to be positive is a positive mindset/identity, coming from someone who used to be quite sadistic.

13. If you're ever stuck in a problem, let it sit in your mind for a while. Think about it, give it time, and your mind will often provide answers in unexpected ways.

14. Never make impulsive emotional decisions. Give yourself at least a day to reflect and see if the decision still feels worth taking.

15. Anger is something you can overcome. It starts with realising that anger over tiny matters often stems from deeper dissatisfaction with life and struggling to accept what life brings. Recognise the toll it takes on you. People often ask how I am so calm; I wish they'd seen me during my childhood and pre-teen years - the angry boy I once was, lol.

16. Be as self-aware as possible; self-awareness is worth investing most of your time in. No one can understand you better than you. Learn to understand your body, mind and personality.

17. Emotions and thoughts are temporary. Give them the importance they deserve, but no more than that.

18. It's okay to remove people from your life.

19. *"If I get there, I will be happy." "If I do that, I will be happy."* I know many people in places that thousands or even lakhs dream of, yet they are unhappy. Happiness is not a place, it's a state of being.

20.When you become grateful, you realise not everyone is as lucky as you are. Don't think twice before offering help.

21. Never say, *"I did this."* You are nothing without the people around you, the opportunities you get, and the environment you are in. Let go of your ego.

22. When you live by strong morals and integrity, people may leave or criticise you. But their behaviour doesn't mean you're wrong - it reflects their discomfort with someone living by higher values than they do.

23. Who am I? is a question worth asking. Spirituality is not just a way of life - it is life.

Love,
Guru Tahanguriya

Life's a book with pages turned,
Lessons lived and wisdom earned.
Each mistake, a teacher true,
Each new day, a chance to grow.

Fall and rise, then walk again,
Learn from loss, embrace the pain.
For every scar and tear we see,
Shapes the soul we're meant to be.

- Unknown

A Letter from Teenage Guru to Present Guru

Dear Guru,

By now, you must have grown so tall. I've got this opportunity to write to my older self, so I'll get straight to the point.

How is Dev? How is our family? Is everyone happy? What about our financial situation? What degree are you pursuing? What career path are you considering? Have you started earning? Have you gained weight?

Did we finally make friends? I feel so lonely here at school.

Most importantly, did we change? You know how weird and different we are. Do you think I'll ever make friends? Will I ever act "normal"?

My mind never stops chattering. I feel like I always have bad luck, nothing ever works out. There's a constant fear inside me about the future and the mistakes I've made in the past. Why am I so negative?

Are you still as angry as I am? Do you still expect a lot from people, only to feel hurt when they don't meet those expectations? Why are people so selfish? Why are they so unfair?

You know, some teachers at school are so biased. They favour a few students and ignore the rest of us like we don't exist. I feel like my potential is being wasted.

Maybe I'm overthinking again.

But one thought keeps haunting me, should I change? Should I stop being good? Should I stop helping others? Because this world doesn't seem to return the kindness, and it feels so self-centred.

Just answer my questions, don't tell me too much about the future. It scares me to death.

I hope you reply, and I hope you reply positively.

Scared,
Guru

A Letter from Present Guru to Teenage Guru

Dear Younger Me,

Yeah, I'm 6 feet tall now, surpassed Dev, and he doesn't like it, haha. The family is doing well, and everyone is happy, just like before. Don't waste too much time worrying about them. If you keep looking into the future, you'll forget that you already have your family with you now. Why wait for happiness? Keep it for every single day.

Financial situations are better than before. I know it's hard for four people to live in a small two-room house, but things will change for the better. In fact, you now have a rented studio. A studio for what? I won't tell you, haha. And yes, you've started earning, but we're just getting started.

Let's not talk about degrees and careers yet, I want you to explore as much as you can, just like I'm doing. Don't limit yourself.

As for weight gain, well, that's still a problem. Please take care of your health and work on your body. Because of your ignorance, I'm suffering now, haha.

You asked if you'll change in the future. The answer is no. You won't change, but you will grow, and there's a difference, dear. You may not understand it now, but you will later.

And yes, we do have friends now, such good friends that you wouldn't believe they exist. So many people love you, more than you can imagine.

You asked if you'll ever act "normal" in the future. Lol, you never will, because you were never abnormal to begin with. Being different from the people around you don't make you weird. You're just an overthinking introvert, kiddo. Start loving yourself.

And no, you're not unlucky or negative, you just need to change your perspective. Now, I'm one of the most positive people around, and I feel incredibly lucky. It's all about mindset. Start reading good books and watching videos that help you learn and grow.

The fear you have of the past and future comes from not valuing the present. Start living. Think less, act more, enjoy the moment, and be content. It will never be "enough" if you keep chasing something. Enough is a mindset. You have enough. You are enough. Realise that.

You're afraid of the mistakes you've made in the past, but let me tell you something, you're going to make plenty more. And that's okay. Those mistakes will make you stronger and wiser.

And no, I'm not as angry as you are. In fact, I'm not angry at all. Stop holding onto an identity that doesn't serve you. Instead, attach yourself to a better one. How about this: *"I am grateful and growing"*?

I know expectations hurt you. And yes, people can be selfish, but what's wrong with that? Aren't you selfish too, in your own way? The problem isn't expecting things from people. The problem is expecting *too much* or relying on them for your happiness. Expecting from others isn't bad, but your happiness should come from within, not from what others do. And remember, if you don't express what you expect, how will people even know? Learn to communicate.

The partiality you see in school? It won't end there. The world is always partial, but in most cases, it favours those who have *value*, those who are *capable*. Stop feeling jealous of classmates who are favoured by teachers. First, accept that they might be working harder than you. And second, if something is unfair, speak up! Don't stay silent out of fear.

And yes, I can see you were overthinking while writing that letter. I still do it sometimes, but now I use my mind to *help* myself, not hurt myself. Learn to sit with your thoughts. Get to know yourself, your strengths, weaknesses, fears; don't run from them. Make yourself your best friend.

You asked if you should change. You talk about it as if it's a choice, haha. Change is inevitable. You *will* change, and so will everyone else. Change is the only constant, and it's a good thing.

And why do you care so much about people who aren't good? Why should their behaviour make you question whether *you* should be good? Are you and they connected in some way? No!

Focus on *your* life, kiddo. Remember, a rose spreads fragrance not to impress others but simply because it is *full* of it. Be so good that goodness flows naturally from you, not forcefully, not as a transaction, but just because it's who you are. Being good shouldn't depend on how others behave.

At the end of your letter, you said, *"Don't tell me about the future if it's not positive, it scares me to death."* Haha. Well, let me tell you about the future, and I won't lie to you.

The truth is: there *is* no future, Guru.

All you have is *now*. The future is just the present that hasn't happened yet. So, live in the present. Love in the present.

Grateful and Content,
Guru

The Gift of Now

The past has gone, the future unknown,
The present is all we truly own.
A fleeting breath, a moment bright,
A chance to live, to love, to light.

- Unknown

Thank You!

Thank you, Maa and Papa, for being my pillars of strength and love. Dev, thank you for standing by my side through every high and low.

To all my relatives and friends, thank you for your unwavering support. And to those rare souls who love me unconditionally and understand me without explanation, you are my greatest blessing.

This book would never have seen the light of day without the love I've received in recent years.

A special thank you to Jugal (Instagram – @jugal.designs) for designing such a stunning cover, your talent gave my words a face.

My heartfelt gratitude to the Twin Bros team, your dedication made this dream possible.

And lastly, to every person whose name I haven't mentioned, there are so many of you who've changed my life in ways you'll never know. The beautiful irony is that many of you don't even know me personally.

Today, I am nothing but deeply, humbly grateful for this life, and for all the love, time, and kindness I've been fortunate enough to receive.

Held by Love, Humbled by Grace,
Guru

Epilogue

Congratulations on making it to the end!

You've completed this journey, and I couldn't be prouder. This book was created with you in mind, packed with everything I believe a Humanities student needs to thrive, both academically and personally.

Whenever you need guidance or just want to revisit what I have shared, this book is always here for you.

I'd love to hear your thoughts! Tag me on Instagram stories or YouTube videos, and let me know how this book has impacted you.

You can reach me anytime:

- Email: tahanguriyaguru@gmail.com

- Instagram: @Guru_Tahanguriya

- LinkedIn: @Guru_Tahanguriya

- YouTube: @TheTwinBros

- X: @GuruTahanguriya

If this book touched you, please consider leaving a review on Amazon, Notion Press or Flipkart. Your support helps others find their way too.

Don't forget to explore our courses and materials on www.thetwinbros.in they're designed to keep you growing.

Thank you, and sending you all my love and encouragement.

Signing off, Guru Tahanguriya

www.ingramcontent.com/pod-product-compliance
Lightning Source LLC
Chambersburg PA
CBHW040809120726
48005CB00012B/1362